Coyote's
POCKET GUIDE
to Connecting Kids with Nature

Ellen Haas &
Lexie Bakewell

ZieBee Media
PORTLAND, OREGON, USA

Coyote's POCKET GUIDE
to Connecting Kids with Nature

Written by
Ellen Haas & Lexie Bakewell

This book is a tool for people who want to connect more deeply with nature, and who want to take groups outside in many different sites and situations.

Edited by Mackenzie Bakewell
Illustrated by Lexie Bakewell & Mackenzie Bakewell
Designed & Published by ZieBee Media - *ZieBee.com*
Photographs by Aaron Baggenstos - *AaronBaggenstos.com*
Cougar Photograph from *www.iStockPhoto.com*
Cover Photograph from *www.Fotolia.com*

ISBN 978-1-7358507-0-2

See more from the authors at:
ZieBee.com/Coyote

ZieBee Media
PORTLAND, OREGON, USA

Table of Contents

Section 5
Raising the Natural IQ

Section 6
Coyote's Ripples

SECTION 1
Nature Connection Education

This book presents "Nature Education as it should be –
mysterious, timeless, hopeful, evocative, and playful."

*(David Sobel, author of Reclaiming the Heart in Nature Education, from
the cover of Coyote's Guide to Connecting with Nature.)*

Chapter 1

An Invitation

Welcome to *Coyote's Pocket Guide to Connecting Kids with Nature*, a basic primer for connecting with nature in your everyday life. This book guides adults who want to take kids outdoors, but who need some help getting started and keeping going.

**We've been told it's exactly
what people are looking for.**

The goal of Coyote Mentoring is to naturalize our children, bringing body, mind, and soul back into a felt connection with nature.

We invite you to adapt your gathering to the natural cycle, to circle up in ceremony and celebration, and to spark curiosity in the hearts of others. Use the framework in this pocket guide to build your own group, your own circle, and adjust the content to exactly what works for you.

Turning the Tide

We have a problem. Kids don't get outside anymore. They don't help on the farm or fish for dinner. They don't kick the can, build tree forts, run and fall down, get lost, get found, and so discover wild beings on their own terms. The children's trails that used to cut across the hills and vales are overgrown or paved or off-limits.

Obesity, attention deficit, diabetes, depression: It's a health problem. It's an environmental problem. It's a spiritual disconnect. It's a cultural tide that needs to be turned.

Coyote Mentoring can turn the tide.

We offer an approach to guiding kids outdoors that sparks curiosity through a sense of adventure, so they hardly know they're learning. It is teaching playfully in your bit of nature.

Coyote is a wily trickster;

Mentor is a god in humble disguise;

Nature is the teacher.

Coyote guides playfully while Mentor leads wisely. You dive in with the kids. You excite them, you explore together, you ask questions, and you do it kindly, safely, and routinely.

Children use their brains that were born to be ever alert to predator and prey, reading Mother Nature's signs. They move their bodies that were designed to survive and thrive running on uneven ground. They absorb vast information. They fall in love with wild nature.

They start wanting to be outdoors. So do their caregivers. Nature grows on them. They learn to love her liveliness. They come to a sense of kinship with her. They care for her.

The tide begins to turn.

Who Are You? *Three Kinds of Users*

This book was written with three groups in mind. It is a wide market, but you have a common vision:

You all want your kids to connect with nature.

Whatever your site, whatever your situation, you can apply the information here to fit your needs.

Families

Parents with children of all ages who want to explore, hike, camp, or just hang out in the local outback. Your activities may manifest in after school programs, homeschooling groups, neighborhood clubs, or backyard buddies, both formal and informal.

Teachers

Instructors, mentors, coaches, tutors who have the opportunity to take students outdoors. You are in charge of children's learning and are aware of the challenges of big groups and school standards. But you are determined to jump all hurdles to get your kids outside so they can experience the benefits of time in nature.

Outdoor Guides

You plan and mentor seasonal outdoor programs that offer everything from summer camps to conquering summits. You lead adventures that build skills, knowledge, courage, and camaraderie – out in parks, fields, trails, and wilderness. Your people may be diverse or at-risk.

Families, Teachers, and Outdoor Guides: This book fertilizes and fires up your intention to raise, teach, and inspire wild-smart, healthy, happy, nature-curious and caring kids.

Who are We? *Coyote's Community*

"Coyote Mentoring" has a long lineage. Lineage means the line of ancestors you come from, your heritage, what your people learned and gave, and what you carry on.

This pocket guide is the offspring of Wilderness Awareness School in the Pacific Northwest.

All our human roots began among ancestors who lived off the land. We are descendants of a global melting pot of people who hunted, gathered, herded, and farmed in a vast variety of environments.

These old roots have been cultivated by Tom Brown Jr, Jon Young, Wilderness Awareness School, and then many programs worldwide who sprouted from them, ever since the 1970s.

All these people formed the core

of the Coyote Mentoring approach.

The Art of Mentoring was taught through experience and apprenticeship outdoors for 15 years before the essence of it was written down in the book *Coyote's Guide to Connecting with Nature*, by Jon Young, Ellen Haas, and Evan McGown.

This monumental manual was the work of a team of Coyote Mentors and it bristles with activities, stories, and coaching.

Published in 2008, it is being used by over 20,000 people in nature schools, environmental centers, forests, farms, and expeditions everywhere.

Coyote's Pocket Guide to Connecting Kids with Nature compacts the big book into practical practices. We have shifted things up and boiled things down to offer a simple framework, with compassion for all your needs.

Purpose of This Guide

This is a portable manual for a broad audience – people who have never heard of the notion "Coyote Mentoring" and people who have, but want an accessible way to put those ideas into action.

It gives you Coyote's tips on how to:

- Tap into child passions
- Alert awareness
- Rouse inquisitiveness
- Harness wild energy
- Harvest excitement
- Savor discoveries

It has six sections that escort you through the basics and suggest a plethora of activities:

- Nature Connection Education
- Coyote Mentoring
- Flowing Activities
- Creating Your Program
- Raising the Natural IQ
- Coyote's Ripples

It coaches you to design an "Invisible School," which is strategically engaging kids in a series of activities that seem like play but are actually lessons in Nature Literacy. Core Routines do the teaching. Mother Nature is the textbook. The outcome is wholehearted connection with, and caretaking of, the land they live on.

If you are a parent, teacher or outdoor guide, consider it a cookbook of ingredients to mix up and heat up. It is not lesson plans, but practices you can adapt to your program, in your place, with your people.

Please come outside and play!

Chapter 2
Connecting with Nature

Imagine a root-bound plant. It's been plugged into that tiny pot until its roots are wound tight and white.

Unplug it. Loosen the roots. Set it in rich soil. Add water and sun. Those roots begin to perk up, unfurl, and send inquiring tendrils outward everywhere.

Our goal is to take kids out of their pots and enrich them with opportunities to connect with nature.

Ease them out of their comfort zones.
Shift their awareness.
Awaken their senses.
Excite their curiosity.
Cultivate their explorations.
Lead them into kinship with wild nature.

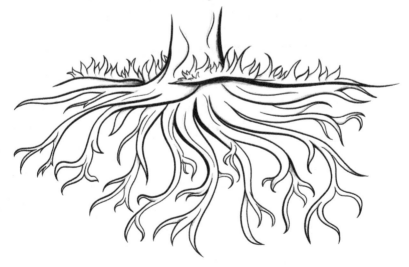

Practicing Core Routines

Connecting with Nature is educational. Simply by playing in the midst of diverse and dynamic processes of nature, children develop knowledge, skills, and abilities.

> *Their bright minds imprint encyclopedias of natural science information.*
>
> *Their active bodies get trained in perception and agility.*
>
> *Their relaxed hearts open into a wondrous sense of natural belonging.*

Nature Connection Education is different from environmental or adventure education. It does, like them, train natural scientists and citizen stewards. It does, like them, empower fitness, courage and leadership. But the Nature Connection taught here has less content and is more playful than some traditional forms of teaching.

How did our indigenous forbearers teach their children? Not in rows in school, but outdoors in mixed age groups, doing routine errands and mundane rituals – greeting the day, collecting plants, scouting animals, telling stories, looking alert, and watching out.

Core Routines of Nature Connection are the key to the Coyote Mentoring teaching method. Both by plan and by happenchance, you guide your adventurers into practicing new habits of awareness. You cultivate a learning culture with regularly repeated routines.

The 13 Core Routines shared in this book simulate some of these cultural practices and all the activities instill one or more of these essential routines (see Chapter 5, p. 30).

Raising the Natural IQ

What we are really doing is raising the Natural IQ. We are teaching the "Naturalist Intelligence," which psychologist Howard Gardner identifies as the base of all the rest of our thinking. It is an ability to perceive patterns in a complex fabric. Such intelligence brightens all other thinking processes.

Natural Intelligence is easy to rouse, because it is already deep in our brain's circuitry. It's what our minds needed to do in our preliterate ancestral days as hunters and gatherers.

The human brain was wired to thrive on relating actively with nature. The brain is most excited while solving problems on the move, quickened by the imperatives of survival. It senses widely. It focuses sharply. It decides quickly. It remembers vividly.

Our modern ways have dimmed our native brain function.

Civilization and technology have turned our attention indoors. When our culture's gaze settles mostly on sheltered and man-made things, attention becomes neurologically entrenched, and we see mostly what we expect to see.

We have atrophied our full range of mental motion. We are missing so much!

To shift this habit takes some deprivation and redirection. Their cell phones often don't transmit out in the wilderness, so kids have to unplug. Then, some deft magic is needed to redirect their attention to the drama of nature.

Watch and you will see: Kids' brains come alive outdoors, they play, get inquisitive, romp like animals, activate the awareness of predator and prey, hunt, explore, and handle terrain and weather like indigenous scouts.

There is a great deal of brain science out there supporting the contention that being in nature is good for improving our overall intelligence.

At the end of this book, we share research and define some standards for Nature Connection Education (see Section 5, p. 107). This includes:

- **The Outdoor Brain**
- **Sensory Wiring**
- **Nature Literacy**
- **Indicators of Nature Connection**

Start with the end, if you like!

Feeling Kinship

A child with natural intelligence will sense when danger is near, will know how to get home after exploring a new place, will be physically more comfortable and agile.

A child who behaves this way will experience safety and friendliness with wild things, will call them by name and be patient and respectful toward them.

Such a child will grow up to feel an intimate sense of kinship with nature.

Kinship is the "biophilia" that scientist E. O. Wilson sees at the neurological heart of our human tendency to affiliate with nature.

Kinship is the intimate knowledge of landscape that the writer Barry Lopez sees as essential to our humanity and fundamental to stewardship of the Earth.

As it evolves, kinship passes through the cycling horizons of life that Sigurd Olsen, conservationist, describes as the childhood wonder, youthful exploration, adult service, and elder pondering of the mysterious Spirit that weaves through the wild.

Connecting with Nature
will turn the tide.

SECTION 2
Coyote Mentoring

Coyote Mentoring calls for combining in yourself the mindsets and skill sets of Coyote and Mentor.

Coyote excites. Mentor guides.
Routines teach. Nature is the textbook.

Chapter 3
Coyote Magic

Imagine Coyote!

Mythical Coyote was the Trickster whose outlandish antics kept creation evolving out of its ruts. He broke the rules, shifted the norm, and saved the day.

He is a lesser god of creation who gets in and out of messes. He is wary, wily, exuberant and easily distracted by scents off the path.

He is quite foolish, and often loses his bets. But he can die and rise again at the snap of a finger.

The trickster has magic. He carries a bundle of tricks in his bag to alert children's senses and point their attention to nature's wonders and puzzles.

The hardest thing for the new Coyote Mentor is to let go of grown-up habits.

For preparation, practice animal faces in the bathroom mirror and whoop loudly while driving. Ask yourself the most elementary questions and think of funny answers. Roll around in the dust and leaves just before starting. Find your inner comedian, actor, and child.

What Children Love

Coyote captures the children's excitement by tapping into their passions with things they love to do.

" Children Love...

Adventuring, discovering, exploring,
hiding, seeking, spying, wandering,
getting lost, getting found.
tasting, and smelling.

Asking questions, being asked questions,
detecting clues, finding answers,
making dares, taking challenges,
teaming up, pairing up,
listening to stories, telling stories,
acting out stories, too.

Drawing, writing, dancing, stomping,
laughing, whistling, clapping, shouting,
throwing things, petting things,
catching little critters, seeing animals close up,
climbing, swinging, splashing, squirting,
racing, chasing, getting muddy.

Imagining, imitating, performing,
show-and-telling, costuming, camouflaging,
decorating, burning, dissecting,
hunting, shooting, carving, making tools,
building forts, whispering, joking,
laughing, hugging, cuddling....

and so much more. "

Children love to play. So Coyote's first trick is to play, down on all fours, stick in mouth, inside kids' passion, at the level of their interests.

Engage them in play, and intervene in all of the following ways.

- **Aim awareness with stories.**
- **Energize it with games.**
- **Harness excitement with song and dance.**
- **Rouse it with challenges.**
- **Gather it with show and tell.**
- **Let it all ferment and do it again.**

Storytelling

Children love stories. They cuddle into them on the lap as toddlers, devour them when they learn to read, and still want them at bedside and fireside as teens; they like stories with pictures, stories with voices, stories that provide metaphors for life and dreams of possibilities.

They get a lot of stories through media, but nothing compares to a home-told story.

So Coyote sometimes starts off with Storytelling. Maybe a sit-down and listen to Grandpa, maybe a promise of today's adventure, maybe a sidelong story – "...Hey, do you want to see if we could do that?"

If you tell a story to start, and then repeat its themes and characters, kids will get entranced. They may chime in with what happened next. They may pick it up and elaborate it in their games.

You can use hints and enticements to catch their interest in your story. "Maybe sometime I'll tell you a story about that." Soon you'll hear, "Can we hear the story now?"

Storytelling seeds their imagination with pictures and dreams and heroics. Coyote does this a lot.

Appreciate Individuality

Children love to be appreciated at eye level, with the grown-up stooping down. They like to be seen for themselves and joined in what they see.

Coyote is alert to each child's distinctive traits. When outdoors with societies of kids, what an opportunity you have to see them in new ways!

Unexpected strengths and weaknesses emerge.

- Get to know your little characters.
- Gauge each child's skills and learning style.
- Watch their edges and challenges.
- Sense what they're proud to know, and what they're scared to find out.
- Gently coax them through their fears.
- Empower their interests and passions.
- Evaluate their learning journeys.

Coyote pushes edges. Coyote has a magic power, the ability to endow special favors, protection fields, and customized errands, all in the service of inspiring each child to reach out and follow where his or her heart sings.

Coyote nips at the edge of comfort zones, creating a bit of healthy stress. Whether a weakness needs strengthening, or a gift needs honing, a challenged mind is alert and therefore learns fast and well.

Sidle up to a hesitant child and whisper encouragement. Say, "I see you are worried about this or that, let me show you a way to manage."

Present Challenges

For the ready ones, be ready yourself with competitions, hunts, quests, or severe cross-questionings!

- **Some kids have information-smarts.** Hand them the field guides and instruments, and put them in charge of nature table displays.
- **Some kids have wild-smarts.** Let them lead expeditions, catch things, craft tools, and manage survival situations.
- **Some kids have imagination-smarts.** Let them invent stories, change the rules of games, imitate, draw, and write.
- **Some just want to move their bodies.** Run, race, tag, and imitate until exhaustion.

The Art of Questioning

Children are naturally curious. They ask all kinds of questions. But guess what? They don't actually want answers. They want you to come down to their level of Wow and What if?

Coyote does not give answers. He lures kids into learning for themselves. The other hardest thing for the new Coyote Mentor to learn is to STOP answering questions. It is not helpful for you to have answers. Answers are not the point. Drag and Brag is boring. Adult information shuts down curiosity

Be Socrates. When they ask, shoot questions back at them, asking them to look more closely with you, asking them to go find out for themselves. Empower their research rather than instruct.

Use Three Levels of questions

- **1: Easy, they already know the answers.** They tell you, proudly.
- **2: Harder, they can find out.** Close examination will yield testable hypotheses.
- **3: Hardest, no one knows,** the lifelong mysteries.

Wrong Answers. It's fun to give them wrong or fantastic answers, just to see what they do. Let them argue. Let them question your authority. *(But make sure you get them corrected before they go home.)*

Give Clues. Coyote, the wild canine out there on the edge of town, leaves hints with a howl, a yip, a track, a scat, or a glimpse of his low-slung tawny tail heading away into the woods.

Point them to Stop! Look! Listen! Then engage them in questioning.

Look Close:

- Who left this sign of being here?
- When in the day and year is it?
- Where are we now?
- Why is this here now?
- How is this connected to this? How does it work?
- How do wild things live here? Could I do that?
- What if? What would it be like to be this?
- How are you like that?

What can you ask about?

Mostly, the art of questioning is the trick of being open to curiosity and wonder.

If you were wild, you would be interested in what you needed to survive – dangerous predators, fascinating prey, safe shelter, larders in times of lack, mating and raising young.

Wild young humans share the instinct. Get them to think like wild animals. Get them to think like a tree!

Remember that there is no such thing as a dumb question. Embody fresh curiosity, get everybody inquisitive, and make contagious games out of quests and hunts.

The 50-50 Principle

Children love a break in routine. Changes wake up their brains, like getting lost and finding something better, or stopping on the way to pick ripe berries, or racing to find shelter from sudden rain.

Coyote follows the 50-50 Principle

When the plan doesn't work or opportunity flies in, Coyote is ready with the 50-50 Principle, which governs educational choices when things change unexpectedly and serendipitously:

> **1:** Plan the whole day.
>
> **2:** But expect to change 50% of it.
>
> **3:** Pack a bag of tricks.

You have a program design, but alas and alert! Attention scatters, dissolves, and refocuses all the time. When some real coyote howls out there in the woods, you'll want to shift the tune and tempo of your lesson. You'll want to change course.

Coyote redirects attention like a magician. Turn their moods and attention from the hand that's rigging the deck to the hand that's pulling the rabbit out.

- If things get hot, grumpy, and tired, take a break.
- When things get dispersed or boring, call them back to center.
- If things get rowdy and crazy, call them in and shoot them out into a rowdier game.
- If there is sadness, give it due attention but move along.
- If there is opportunity, pack up and chase it.

Coyote's Plan?

Adjust and Adapt!

Raise a Village

Children love being raised in a Village, with its familiar faces and bustling novelties, where chickens roam around pecking, while cousins gather at the water pump, where all the grown-ups keep their eyes on all the kids, and every child can find a personal mentor.

It takes a village to raise a child. Coyote's a fool, but what he knows deep and well is wise and true:

> A child needs many mentors – siblings,
> teachers, peers, heroes, parents, elders,
> and chance encounters.

It's easier with others. If you've got a bunch of kids outdoors, you NEED another competent grown-up along for emergencies, or just for corralling and potty-breaks. Teaching with a partner or a team gives you breathing space, perspective, and inspiration.

Coyote Recruits!

He scouts around at night and drags in extra grown-ups to come along for adventures. Enlist other parents from the neighborhood, an aide at school, or a team of staff at camp.

Experienced teens make great scouts, hiding in trees and ambushing! Or helping with fire and shelter building. Or bringing up the rear of the hike.

Moms and Dads become Aunties and Uncles, caring for the whole tribe as their own children. They can support the gathering and greeting, and contribute diversity to all the Coyote Mentoring.

Older people and government officials become Elders, treated respectfully and working with individuals on projects. They can come in and out, bring in expertise, or just ask curious guest questions.

Coyote hangs out. Coyote may get these recruits involved by sheer laziness: starting late and lingering long, so that a village of kids' friends and families begin to attach.

Give everyone things to do. Get the village involved in checking out the items you've brought back to the nature tables, sit around the fire circle to share story of the day, build up Home Base into a nice camp with adult help, sing a song together, eat together, work on crafts together.

Enlist experts. And if some of your Village Aunties, Uncles, and Elders are accomplished naturalists, artists, musicians, or story-tellers, give them a little stage time. Get them to teach their skills or tell their stories by surrounding them with children eager to learn.

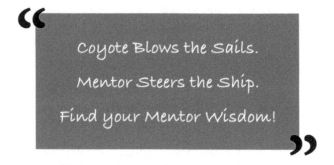

> Coyote Blows the Sails.
>
> Mentor Steers the Ship.
>
> Find your Mentor Wisdom!

Chapter 4
Mentor Wisdom

Imagine Mentor!

Mentor is the mystical helmsman in Homer's timeworn Odyssey, a god disguised as a servant who rudders the ship across turbulent seas to deliver a young man into his destiny!

The disguised tillerman is a humble background character who puts a lot of vigilance, navigation, muscle-in-a-crisis, and godly grace into guiding the voyage.

Mentor is the strong, loving, skilled and wise adult companion on the kids' journey. Coyote is only his foolish sidekick. And a Coyote Mentor embodies both.

Mentor steers the ship. Find your Mentor wisdom!

Steer the Course

Guide your wards toward their destinies. Set up a string of games as an Invisible School (see below), where the kids don't know they're learning.

Plan a course of things to do – with the kids you have, in the place you are – that teaches Nature Connection and Natural Intelligence in all its facets, without scrunched up effort.

Invisible School

This idea offers an interesting new perspective on school design. The teaching part is camouflaged in a **fresh arrangement of the course or curriculum.**

You know in your Mentor's Mind, that you are subtly steering them into your plan for connecting with nature. You do have learning objectives. But you introduce them as if they were talking points in an interview instead of material to cover in a curriculum.

Plan a program adapting the tools described further along in this book. Flow of Activities suggests a sequence of activities. Creating your Program offers a basic scheme for planning.

Gather participants, scope your site (location), pick up your inner Coyote on the roadside, and begin.

But then step back to the stern. This gives the kids a chance to lead, giving nature a chance to teach, and giving Coyote a chance to do his luring.

Watching from the background as kids play, you can keep a sharp eye on the energy of the group and the kids in it and you can stay one step ahead of it, like a football coach calling plays.

Are they learning the elements of Natural Intelligence? Using their Senses, practicing Core Routines? Are they challenged? Is there a brightness in them?

Watch from behind and give Coyote the nod to nudge their learning.

This can be done by asking a question to pique their curiosity or by sending them out on a new adventure.

Expand Comfort Zones

While Coyote is tripping them up, Mentor protects children at their edges.

Putting your foot down, off the pavement, at any time of day, in all kinds of weather, can be truly scary.

Wilderness is outside the civilized comfort zone.

Cultural fears abound. We want railings, security, guaranteed gadgets, germ-free worlds. Fear and reluctance are clues to the edges of children's comfort zones.

Facing fear outdoors enhances health and fitness. Exposure to wild and unpredictable nature is good medicine. It creates common sense, and shows kids how resilient they are.

Allow yourself beyond your own comfort zone. Assure yourself that the children will be safer for facing some outdoor challenges than they will be if they don't. And you will be, too.

Get them to know they are basically safe in a beautiful, changing, unified natural environment. They belong. Nature loves them, if they take her by the right handle.

Tease and cajole them out of the box
- The box of fears they have inherited.
- The box of being plugged-in indoors.
- The box of their perceived inabilities, emotional hurts, and confusions brought from their lives.
- The box of a potted plant's limited awareness.

Observe and guide kids gently beyond their fears
- See resistance as your starting point.
- Meet their fears with your curiosity.
- Dispel old wives' tales. Show when it's safe.
- Capture their attention with new things.
- Shift them into adventures that become the Story of the Day.

Keep Them Safe & Harmless

Mentor harnesses the wild energy that Coyote stirs up and holds the ship on course.

Take on a mindset and ripen a skill set to steer your precious wards to be safe and practice harmlessness. Here are some sets of common sense advice. See them as checklists.

Hazards

A hazard is a problem that might happen. Its risk is measured by the extent of damage that could result if it does. Calculate your risk, make wise choices, but go ahead and prepare to deal with facing some consequences of hazards.

> **There is no such thing as bad weather,
> only inappropriate clothing!**

Warnings

- **Never take a risk you can't handle.**
- **Know how to never get lost.**
- **Practice basic medicine.**

Be Prepared

- **Preview** your staff, volunteers, and kids for suitable behavior and medical concerns.
- **Survey your site** before leading people into it.
- **Agree** to respect boundaries, human and natural, and enforce these boundaries early and clearly.
- **Keep track of time.** Leave when you said. Get home when you promised.
- **Monitor needs** for water, rest, privacy, and attention.
- **Learn and teach local hazards**, and how to deal with them: plants, animals, terrain, weather.
- **Check Equipment.**

Etiquette

Stay on the trail in public parks or else find welcoming private land, vacant lots, or ditches to wander more freely. Make friends with landowners, park rangers, and farmers.

When collecting, pick something only when there are a lot of them around. Don't pull plants up by the roots when all you want is a flower. When you turn over a log or rock, replace it. Try not to trample.

If you handle an animal, make sure your hands are inoffensive: don't give it your smell. If you pick it up, return it to the spot you found it or hide it in a safe place to rest and recover from the stun of meeting you.

Practice harmlessness: Don't randomly kill things.

Practice leaving it better than you found it: Cart home other people's litter. Undo your own shelter buildings. Put your fire out. Restore wounded land.

Greet strangeness with curiosity. Meet new things gently, at their level. As in Avatar, say, "I see you."

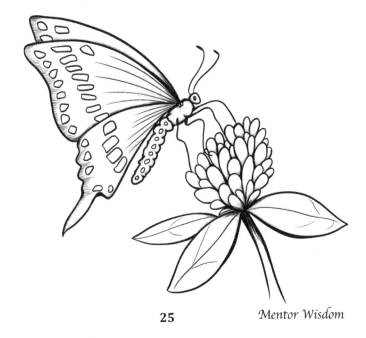

25

Social Agreements

Make clear agreements.

Early on, before they get feral, sit down with your kids – whether one or many – and have a little chat about being nice to each other, learning together, and doing nature no harm.

Make some community agreements. Be prepared to enforce rules. Start out as a Drill Sergeant.

Where can you go?
- Stay this close to the group. Stay inside these boundaries. Follow this map.
- Set rules for staying together, calling in, buddy checks.

What can you do?
- Leave no trace. Leave it better than you found it.
- Take care of yourself. Hydrate. Eat. Rest. Use your sunscreen.

Principles for Peaceful Communities
- Settle down, get peaceful, get grateful.
- Appreciate others. Listen to all points of view. Support and encourage.
- Come to agreement for the good of the whole.

Principles for Reconciliation
- If you have disagreements, talk them out using your best words.
- Listen hard. Keep trying. Find common ground.
- Forgive and forget. Let wounds heal.
- Reconcile.

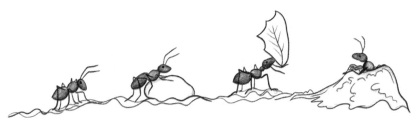

Mentor Wisdom

Harness Wild Energy

Kids, when unleashed, can wreak havoc.

Things emerge. They find cool sticks as walking canes, then make them into swords. Children used to cooperative games find themselves in awkward competitions. Kids used to control and regimen find themselves free with wide boundaries.

Emotions rise in strange outdoor places – fears and terrors, homesickness, left-outness, worn-outness. Excitement and awesome discovery ignite outbursts. All this opens volcanic vents, and kids do crazy things.

Consider this image.

We have three parts of our brain:

- **The Thinking** brain that makes civilized decisions.
- **The Emotional** brain that feels happy/sad.
- **The Reptile** brain that instinctively fights, flees, or freezes.

Kids in their comfort zone think clearly. Sharing around Home Base at the end of the day is a good place to debrief the thrills and chills and group dynamics in a safe, casual, thinking way.

Kids exploring the edges of their comfort zones are in their Emotional Brain. The activities of the outing will focus their stress into emotions out on their sleeves. Kids playing are like puppies in training; let them have their spats and learn positively from them.

Kids who go too far too fast can find themselves in Reptile Brain. They fight, flee, or freeze.

> **"When two Velocipedes are fighting,**
> **the mentor becomes Tyrannosaurus Rex."**
>
> *- Sol Doran -*

Mentor Wisdom

Stop the fight, split out the perpetrators, and take them away for a walk with you.

Let them vent, mimic their reptile anger – acknowledge that you "get it," – and ease them down into how they feel, then empathize with that.

Only then will you get through to their thinking brain, that "This is not acceptable behavior," this is not what the group agreed to, we need to be safe out here together, so here are the rules, the terms of your probation, and a process for reconciliation.

As the wise writer D.H. Lawrence wrote:

> When we escape turning like squirrels in our cages,
>   and get into the forests again, ...
> Cool, unlying life will rush in,
> And passion will make our bodies taut with power,
> We shall stamp our feet with new power
> And old things will fall down.
> We shall laugh,
> and institutions will curl up like burnt paper.

Humor in Hardship

Children outdoors will encounter adversity and get into crises.

A Coyote Mentor sees crisis as opportunity and manages it with humor. Comedy, ultimately, takes us to a happy ending.

Hilarity purges fear. If you can find something funny in an adverse experience, you will remember it with fondness.

Absolutely, the funniest and funnest challenge we all face is jumping kids over the hurdles that beset young growing mammals.

Obstacles you meet will end up being the favorite Stories of the Day. Great humor will come in as an afterthought from slugging through some kind of mud together.

> The ability to see something amusing in
> scary, difficult, and awkward times is a
> gift of grace. Open yourself to laughter
> when it's the best medicine.

As the adult in charge, manage the crisis yet keep things educational. Don't stamp a crisis down and take control, but invite the kids to handle it.

Coach the kids to take it on as a solvable problem.

Watch what happens. Read its messages: what not to do again. Slowly, the humor of their situation dawns on them and they develop wisdom.

If it's a human crisis, child unhappiness, weakness, fear, pain, left-outness, you can still manage it with humor.

Support resilience.
Find grace.
Give love.
Draw out a smile.

Chapter 5
Cultivate Core Routines

Coyote Mentoring is all directed at practicing the "Core Routines of Nature Connection." These are essential habits that harness the natural inclinations of children outdoors. They redirect attention and awaken awareness.

Set each one up by doing it once well, then repeat and repeat in little ways until your group becomes a learning community that practices these drills all the time.

The Core Routines of Nature Connection are practices:

- Things you do every day in every way.
- Things you do with kids outdoors whenever and wherever.

Imagine a habit you can't wait to practice because you know it feels good after. You pursued it and have become familiar with it.

You practiced cello. You trained for soccer. You raised kids. You got a PhD. You became a carpenter, a teacher. You instilled routines with care.

Now they are lifelong habits that kick in whenever they are needed.

Each Core Routine for Nature Connection awakens a kind of "mindfulness," an attention toward nature. These habits of mind are all tendrils of the Natural Intelligence.

Here are our favorite 13 Core Routines. There are many more depending on the culture you live in. Think of what your own are.

1. Sit Spot *(see p. 32)*
   The practice of sitting in nature regularly at the same place.

2. Story of the Day *(see p. 33)*
   Sharing your finds and recounting the highlights of your day.

3. Expanding Awareness *(see p. 34)*
   Quieting your mind by awakening and expanding your senses.

4. Imitating Animals *(see p. 35)*
   Imagining and acting out animals' movements and behavior.

5. Questioning & Tracking *(see p. 36)*
   Looking for clues and asking questions to learn more about mysteries you encounter.

6. Wandering *(see p. 37)*
   Taking time to wander with no agenda, to follow your curiosity.

7. Mapping & Orienting *(see p. 38)*
   Paying attention to the directions, creating maps and knowing where you are in the landscape.

8. Field Guides *(see p. 39)*
   Browsing and searching through books to identify and learn about things that capture your attention.

9. Keeping Journals *(see p. 40)*
   Regularly recording your experiences in a journal by drawing, mapping and writing.

10. Survival *(see p. 41)*
   Practicing basic outdoor survival skills and techniques.

11. Mind's Eye Imagining *(see p. 42)*
   Looking deeply to create a mental image to use later.

12. Listening for Bird Language *(see p. 43)*
   Learning the tones of voice and erratic behaviors of birds to better understand what is going on in the landscape.

13. Thanksgiving *(see p. 44)*
   Expressing gratitude for the abundance, beauty, and presence of the natural world and all who live in it.

Sit Spot

Sit Spot is still, quiet, and alone.

Find one place in your natural world that you visit all the time and get to know it as your best friend.

Sit alone quietly there. Do so often.

Create time for Sit Spot – anything from a moment of silence, to a game of hide and seek, to a regular five-minute sit, to an overnight vigil. Grow a habit of taking time out to be quiet and alone in nature.

Let Sit Spot be a place where you learn to sit still and invisible with all your senses alert.

With a little patience and an empty mind, you can tune into a constant many-species conversation around your Sit Spot that changes through the days and seasons. If you sit still, the animals come to you. This will become a place of intimate connection.

❝ *To look at any thing,*
If you would know that thing,
You must look at it long:
To look at this green and say
"I have seen spring in these
Woods," will not do – you must
Be the thing you see:
You must be the dark snakes of

Stems and ferny
plumes of leaves,
You must enter in
To the small silences
between the leaves,
You must take your time
And touch the very peace
It issues from. **❞**

John Moffitt

Story of the Day

Story of the Day is recalling vividly.

Tell the story of your day with others. Let a story circle be an ending routine after shared adventures. Invite everyone's voice. Show and tell all the vivid stories.

What did we do today? What was funny? What was awesome? What was hard? Draw group maps and compare notes. Act out what happened. Show what you found.

Kids love sharing their excitement and wonder.

Saying it out loud with others echoes long afterward in a child's memory. A mentor's listening and questioning can draw out learning from an experience that otherwise might have been easily forgotten. A peer group's respectful attentiveness and applause lifts a child's heart and courage.

 Natural history writers are storytellers. Scientists are storytellers.

Scientists live and die by their ability to depart from the tribe and go out into an unknown terrain and bring back, like a carcass newly speared, some discovery and lay it in front of the tribe; and then they all gather and dance around it.

There is fundamentally no difference from a Paleolithic campsite celebration.

E.O. Wilson

Expanding Awareness

Expanding Awareness is stretching the sensory mind.

Use and expand all your senses as fully as you can, one at
a time and together. See, hear, touch, smell, taste.
Stretch Out! Look Alert! Pay attention!

Use the five senses intentionally by looking closely, gazing
widely, hearing keenly, smelling the landscape, feeling the
textures, sensing the weathers, listening for bird language.

Infuse the whole outing with a pepper of questions and
check-it-outs, quizzes and scavenger hunts, that engage
the senses actively and imprint images vividly.

> *There is an intimate reciprocity to
> the senses; as we touch the bark
> of a tree, we feel the tree touching
> us; as we lend our ears to the
> local sounds and ally our nose to
> the seasonal scents, the terrain
> gradually tunes us in turn.*
>
> David Abram,
> Spell of the Sensuous

Imitating Animals

Imitating Animals is empathetic exercise.

Imitate any and all animals, physically, mentally, and emotionally in their movements, behaviors, and personalities.

Be wild! Imagine what it's like to warm up like a chickadee, sniff like a dog. Put your body in animal shapes and imitate their moves and different ways of perception. Be the character of a rock, or a tree growing. Be anything wild, and develop an affectionate empathy with it.

Establish a habit of fox-walking and owl-eyes as you walk along, dart into shelter and camouflage, creep upon with feline stealth. Study walks, gallops, and bounds and move like that. Dance and howl.

> *Kingfishers: they make a hellacious noise, blast and rattle before them, so the whole world knows they're coming. Rest on a branch over water with their big bills, suddenly dive. Hit the water and shoot their wings back to propel themselves that extra jolt forward. Tom would say, "Let's go be kingfishers." We'd climb on the rock and dive straight down and try to catch a fish with our faces.*
>
> Jon Young

Questioning & Tracking

Questioning and Tracking is inquisitive focus.

Track everything. Learn to see invisible things from the trail
that all action leaves around itself.

Follow clues to investigate:
Who, What, When, Where, How?
Wonder Why.

Become a child and explore under rocks. Become a scientist and test hypotheses. Become a detective and solve a mystery.

Tease up inquisitiveness. Arouse inquiry. Do research. Push questions until they yield answers. Inspire close observation driven by real curiosity.

> *A naturalist is someone who pays attention. Paying attention brings you into intimate contact with the world. To be a naturalist you must be curious, observe actively and closely, describe and identify what is before you, take good notes, look for patterns in all scales, reflect on where you've been and what you've seen, and immerse yourself in the natural world. For a naturalist – intimacy is everything. We must dive deep and immerse ourselves...*
>
> Saul Weisberg

Wandering

Wandering is being here now.

Slow down and rest. Wander through the landscape without destination, agenda, or future purpose.

Be present in the moment. Go off-trail and off-leash wherever curiosity leads and rules allow.

This is the habit to break habits. Take a break. Wander off-course. Make time for unstructured time, undirected play.

Then let things take their fluid course. Enjoy the current. Let it be. When you let it under your skin, then you begin.

> **"** *What, to curious kids, is less vacant than a vacant lot? ...A creek bed, a weedy field... are places of initiation, where the borders between ourselves and other creatures break down, where the earth gets under our nails and a sense of place gets under our skin.* **"**
>
> Robert Michael Pyle,
> The Thunder Tree

Mapping & Orienting

Mapping and Orienting is noticing where you are.

Picture your landscape from a bird's eye view and draw
its maps. Put in East, South, West, and North.

Sketch in significant landmarks. Etch maps in the sand
to show the route of your adventures.

Orient to the sun and how its light and heat affects the turn
of your place's days and seasons, its plants, animals, and
you.

Practice mapping the compass directions. Where is West?
Where did the sun set? Which slope gets more sun? Where
is moss thick?

Navigate trails with a topographical map in mind. Learn to
use a compass. Practice getting lost and found.

> ❝ *...Remember a time when you journeyed
> on foot over hundreds of miles, walking
> fast and often traveling at night, travel-
> ing nightlong and napping in the acacia
> shade during the day, and these stories
> were told to you as you went. In your trav-
> els with an older person you were given a
> map you could memorize, full of lore and
> song, and also practical information. Off
> by yourself you could sing those songs to
> bring yourself back.* ❞
>
> Gary Snyder

Field Guides

Field Guides is identification and naming.

**Browse through field guides as treasure chests
of knowledge that fill up the vacuum
of your curiosity about nature.**

Field Guides are traveling companions, nature table resources, and rainy day picture books, full of photos and
drawings, clues and maps, arrows and anecdotes and
explanations. They're written by great naturalists. They
teach scientific language.

Keep some handy. Bring them out opportunely. Invite
browsing, Compare your sightings and specimens with the
books' pictures and ranges. Take up sketching and using
magnifying lenses.

> *Think of field guides as wise elders who
> offer gems that answer questions, tell sto-
> ries, and give clues. Curl up with them on
> your lap and let them lead you on a jour-
> ney that broadens your horizon.*

Lexie Bakewell

Keeping Journals

Keeping Journals is putting experience into words.

Keep a regular record, in words and drawings, of your experiences outdoors. Keep dated logs, sketches, captions, and comments that describe your finds and stories.

Keep it up though all the seasons until it becomes a habit you can't live without.

Journaling, sketching, and collecting are ways to honor the magic in a day. Take quiet time out to reflect, put experience into words, show-and-tell your finds, draw perception into sketches, and log notes for stories.

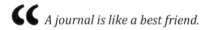 *A journal is like a best friend.*

> *A place to share exciting adventures, bounce around ideas, try out poetry, sketch things, and capture memories you want to remember and share.*
>
> *Best of all, a journal can be a pathway to connecting with your inner self.* **"**

Lexie Bakewell

Survival

Survival is primal passion.

Interact with the natural world around you on a survival basis, including all the basic human needs: shelter, water, fire, food, tools, clothing, and art.

Put kids out in the elements to live a while. They will grow a realization that basic comforts are within reach once they build some skills.

They will look back with delight on freezing wet nights and near-death experiences and dangerous animal sightings! They will always be comfortable outdoors. Survival will feel like thrival.

> **"** *Without weariness there can be no real appreciation of rest, without hunger no enjoyment of food; without the ancient responses to the harsh simplicities of the kind of environment that shaped mankind, a man cannot know the urges within him.* **"**
>
> Sigurd Olson,
> Open Horizons

Mind's Eye Imagining

Mind's Eye Imagining is thinking in images.

Use and strengthen your imagination by snapping pictures of images that your mind gathered from the intense focus of all the senses.

Close your eyes, and recall an image with your mind's eye. Sketch from memory and check back and revise. Tell your story, and cross-question it. Thus, you learn by heart.

Go further into empathy. Imagine what it would be like to be an animal or a plant. Feel the fur, bones, muscles, veins, the acute senses; feel the endurance of a tree who only stands still.

Make art: Look close with a magnifying lens, look far with telescoping eyes, frame scenes, photograph closeups, paint with colors.

" *Imagination enlarges vision, stretches the mind, challenges the impossible. Without imagination, thought comes to a halt.* **"**

Wilfred Peterson

Listening for Bird Language

Listening for Bird Language is intuition.

Be still and listen.

Quiet down and crane your ears and eyes to notice the tattletale voices and gestures of birds and other animals, including humans. What message do you hear?

Walk carefully and quietly, creating as little disturbance as a human can. Listen for quick rustlings in the grass, twitters of alarm, distant honking flights.

At deeper levels, this routine is about emotional intelligence, the ability to sense the mood of people and place, to feel safety and danger, to respond with awareness, respect, and empathy.

At deepest levels, it is about stillness and being present to the soft breezes of the spirit.

> *If the animals can do it, you can too. You can learn to listen to the first hints of alarm, and you can also prevent the alarm. It's very similar to learning to walk by one of those motion-detector lights without flipping it on. There are motion detectors in the forest that read your intent, that read your body language, that know your mind and pass the message on as you approach.*
>
> Jon Young

Thanksgiving

Thanksgiving is an attitude of gratitude.

Find in yourself a grateful heart and express real thanks for any and all aspects of nature and life.

Nature has always followed the path of resilience. To lift up and move forward! To be glad to be alive! When you give thanks, you feel this.

Every day in every way, lift your heart to notice what you love and say it aloud. Try to begin every episode with excitement and appreciation. Give nods of praise as you go about your day.

This is the beginning and the end of connecting with nature, simply paying appreciative attention.

> *Be genuine.*
> *Grow soft and lift your heart to*
> *feel grateful.*
> *Stop everything and listen when*
> *someone has a story to tell.*
> *Take time to say "thank you."*
> *Discover the extraordinary in the*
> *ordinary and admire it.*
>
> Ellen Haas

SECTION 3
Flowing Activities

Here's the Meat!
Here's what you DO with kids outdoors.

This section introduces a natural flow of activities that you can pick among to move your kids along. Each section starts with "What children love."

Each chapter is packed with tips and tricks. You can browse it or study it. Glimpse possibilities. Say to yourself, "Hey, I could do that." Envision how these activities could work for you in your place, with your weather, your vegetation, and your people.

The 8 Flowing Activities

1. **Home Base** *(see p. 47)*
   A landing place for gathering, re-grouping, and sharing.

2. **Greet & Gather** *(see p. 50)*
   Corralling and settling in a group with games, activities and stories.

3. **Energize Awareness** *(see p. 55)*
   Active games and structured play to energize and start the day.

4. **Forays** *(see p. 63)*
   Adventures and expeditions out into nature.

5. **Wandering** *(see p. 70)*
   Unstructured time to take a break and relax from focused attention.

6. **Show & Tell** *(see p. 72)*
   Taking turns to share stories and finds from the day's outings.

7. **Still, Quiet, Alone** *(see p. 77)*
   This is Sit Spot, time to be still, expand senses and get to know the place as a friend.

8. **Ceremony** *(see p. 85)*
   Opening and closing the gathering, celebrating passages and accomplishments, and giving gratitude.

Creating Your Program, (Section 4, p. 89) gives a framework to plan and implement your events and adventures.

Chapter 6
Home Base

Children love a cozy warm familiar play-filled home, circled by parents and guests who like to hang with them.

Consider Home Base a place where you meet and greet before and after your nature outings. You eat lunch, return to it. It's the home you fix up, and invite visitors to. It's the village gathering place.

If you build it, they will come. Scout out a gathering place outdoors. It can be a clearing near your home, in the schoolyard, or in the park. In some cases, you will bring your supplies and "rebuild it" each time if you're not able to keep your Home Base set up (such as in a public park).

Set it up to be attractive. Make it captivating, and then capture the kids in this corral!

Over time, build it into a Village, where kids and their extended families hang out, replete with a fire pit, stations for projects, and a nature museum. Or an overnight camp.

It helps if potable water, toilets, and parking are nearby.

Or, equally, build an indoor "outdoor space" in your classroom or home and bring natural things back to it. Add a tent, an aquarium, raise a guinea pig.

The following are three elements that can help you begin building your Home Base.

Circle Center

Circles of people have gathered around the fire since before Neanderthal turned to Homo Sapiens. The circular seating allows equal access and importance to everyone. The teacher is only part of the circle.

The fire in the middle lights up everyone's faces and gestures, and people tell their stories to the center where the heat and glow is.

Wherever you are, however informal, gather around a circle and put a spark in the center (even if that is just a bright flower).

Orientation

Orient to the Compass Directions.
Remember where the sun is at during different times of day here at Home Base. Figure out where are East, South, West, and North, and install four stump table-tops to mark the four directions.

Invite a kid-drawn Map of where you are.
Provide props: Lay out an open sketchpad and spread out some pencils. Unfold a contour map. Open a terrain-from-an-airplane app. Carry a phone and map your waypoints.

Nature Tables

Set up some table-tops here in your Home Base, at your leisure. On top of these, put out things you find. Gradually curate "little altars everywhere" for Show and Tell.

Prepare a Resource Table.
Depending on the size and scope of your program, these Nature Tables can be humble or extravagant.

- Bring in some field guides and lay them out at kid-level.
- Gather skulls and leaves, feathers and bones, bird nests and natural musical instruments.
- Set them out – on the table, on top of the stumps, in the center.
- Include magnifying and dissecting tools.

If you have an ongoing Village, like a classroom or campsite, furnish it with Nature Tables and craft niches. As kids add their finds and arts, these can grow into full-scale science labs or nature museums.

Chapter 7

Greet & Gather

Children love coming together in a place filled with children. They love greeting old buddies and eyeing new ones.

But they're a little scared and want to watch first. Or they need to run off their nervousness, or they need to show off.

They love the fol-de-rol of centering up but it takes Coyote Magic to bring a group of kids to center in the wide outdoors.

Coyote's way to shape a Group into a Gathering is an array of Greeting and Gathering rituals.

In canine, it's smelling rear ends and bowing to play. In bird, it's flock calls and dawn choruses. In human, it's greeting and gathering routines.

Stretching Games

When kids arrive at the start of an outing, you can get them busy and comfortable by setting up simple games.

They need to stretch out, like a cat waking up, twitching muscles and whiskers. Or a dog at the beginning of a walk, all smelling and prancing.

Gather with them into an Animal Stretches warm-up circle to get your heartbeats started.

- Shiver like a chickadee
- Stretch like a cat
- Balance like a heron
- Shake off water like a dog

Gather those who want a game into a small easy-to-learn game, such as Simon Says or Tag. Encourage newcomers.

Circles

Children instinctively understand the call of circles. The Circle is what we start with, come into often. Calling a Circle is a routine you can rely on to get everyone united.

CAW!!! CAW!!! Catches their attention. Use it to say, "Gather back together now." Everyone passes it on in a cacophony. Five-minute warnings are helpful.

Then entice them with a catchy game. "If you can hear me now, stand on one leg... If you can hear me now, touch your nose... If you're here now, get toe to toe... "

Start up a song, a little dance. Or create a hilarious commotion. Outsiders get interested. The group gathers into a circle.

Respectful Listening

Teach them to listen when they are gathered in circles. Listen to you, listen to each other, use their own best words. Explain to them your rules and standards for respectful listening. Practice learning the rules in a lighthearted way.

Be consistent in enforcing protocols from the get go. This is like teaching a dog to Sit! If you let a child bully you, you lose authority that you have to regain. If you let a child talk over other children, you are telling the quieter child that he or she is less worthy of being heard.

Slow down! Sometimes you'll have to intervene to remind about listening. Whenever necessary, take the time out to remind everyone of the protocols.

Be firmly loving. Assume a matter-of-fact, non-judgmental tone with children.

Names

Children want people to know their names.
Naming a name is empowering. It means you know who I am.

Naming Names
Do mnemonics to register and remember names. Use them often in call-outs and appreciations. Play name-repetition games.

Nature Names
Surprise their expectation. Rename them with Nature Names. "What's your favorite animal?" "That's your name for now." Or pick a prepared name tag out of a hat: dog, fern, banana slug.

You pick one too, then everyone calls each other by these names. With new people, they're easier to remember. With old friends, they rename for the occasion.

As time goes on, this Nature Name takes on a leading fascination. **"Why am I called that?"**

A Story to Start

Children love Story Circle, when the grownup tells the story.

Imagine YOU telling stories with kids crowded around your knees. Here's where you channel Coyote. Tell a good one.

Go a little wild. When the storyteller gets into it, and the story comes alive, the audience gets sucked in.

Coyote is an entrancing storyteller. He remembers something and just gets going on telling about it, and as he goes, the story gets bigger and bigger. He:

> Tells you how things smell and taste,
> Imitates what he's talking about,
> Plays his crowd,
> Fascinates his audience.

Engage them in the story.
Call on kids to respond through little interactive asides. After a few times, you can build up a gospel choir of call and response.

> "And then, what do you think Bear said?"
> They all growl.

Stories told at the beginning settle in and become the warp and weave of your outing. So, pick a story to tell that sets the theme and challenge you want.

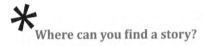

Where can you find a story?

- **Your own recent** everyday stories in glistening detail, what excited you today.
- **Your own most heroic stories.** Mission driven. Obstacles overcome. Challenge met. Applause.
- **YouTube, TV and movies,** great bits retold.
- **Amazing hero stories** from legend and literature. Worldwide. Male and female.
- **Nature factoids.** Astonishing eyeballs, leaping feats, mating tricks.
- **Animal advisories.** Aesop's fables. Coyote lessons with thought-provoking morals.
- **Ancestral lore.** History, personal and regional. Who lived here originally, who hunted, mapped, settled, bought-and-sold this land?

Singing and Dancing

Children love singing and dancing. It happens spontaneously. Yowls of joy. Pack-cries of laughter. Rap rhymes, candy commercials. If it's simple and repetitive, they can sing and dance to it.

Sing to become a group.

Everybody can sing, even YOU. Learn one short song. Invite harmonics. Hike to a pace-setting chain gang song. Sing songs with nature names.

If you can really sing or play a guitar, sing it out. Pick strong words full of nature facts.

Everybody can dance. Dance together, inside a singing circle, moving as one, to a beat, for a while.

Create percussion by banging anything together. That usually gets people moving with a degree of uniformity. Teach your drummers to go loud or soft.

Teach a rhythm dance. "You put your right toe in, you put your right toe out. You do the hokey pokey and turn it all about."

There are many possibilities, only limited by your inhibitions.

Thanksgiving

Even irreverent Coyote takes a moment at daybreak and dusk to give an exuberant yip upward, celebrating his good fortune to be alive in this wild world, calling on a good day ahead.

Children love saying what they love. Saying out loud to listening friends what caught their attention, made them happy today, what was funny, what was exciting.

Lift hearts into appreciating each other and all the natural things around them. Give thanks out loud.

Love the extraordinary in the ordinary and call attention to it by expressing your delight throughout the day.

Gather in the beginning and take a moment do an opening circle of thanks. You can also do it when something wonderful happens. And give thanks again just before you part at the end of day.

Depending on your ceremonial space, Thanksgiving can be manifest as an everybody-says-something circle, or a popcorn of contributions, a somber prayer, or a group yelp.

Chapter 8
Energize Awareness

Children love just plain play that energizes bodies and expands awareness. Active games all perk up their bodies and brains to be supple and sharp. They're growing instinct, agility and alertness, so it's simply fun to use those capacities!

The next activities emphasize high energy and also quiet awareness games, but these two aspects are so intertwined that they fit into a big bag of tricks with each other.

Energizing Games

Physical games are Coyote's jump starter. You can do these even before saying "Hello!"

A little playful competition makes games thrilling. It wakes up strategies for fighting and fleeing. That's how the puppies learn their bodies.

Imitate Animals
Children love acting like animals.
Kids get into the mindset of animals by walking with their footsteps.

Appreciate how wild beings move.
Start right off by imitating animals in your body movements. Study them. Emulate them. Teach quiet feet, uplifted knees, leaping power. Also, trees in storm, water flowing, granite cracking…

Acrobatics: Contort your body to jump like a rabbit, with hind legs landing in front of front legs, or run low like a lizard with bowed-out elbows and knees.

Animal Charades: Act out the voices of birds, the eating style of deer, the wind in a dust storm, and see who can guess who you are. Do it as skits.

Imagine what it would be like to see, hear, smell, taste with animal capability. Imagine echolocating like a bat, expending the energy of a hummingbird, moving as slow as a snail. View the world from an ant's perspective.

Camouflaging, scouting, sneaking, hiding, hunting and ambushing tend to develop around the practice of imitating animal strategies.

Coyote Trickster: This is YOUR animal form to practice! Be a wild canine, alert, stealthy. Play, question, and improvise. Yip occasionally. Collapse in exhaustion. Rise again!

Run and Race

Kids love to run full out, to dart and dodge, and count coup.

Ready, Set, Go:
Jump up suddenly and challenge a group to run from a start to finish line…

- While yelling
- Over hurdles
- Through a gauntlet
- Evading capture
- Like an elephant

Use these games throughout: At the beginning to get rid of nervous energy. After sitting and focused activity. On Demand!

Tag and Count Coup

Tag starts as small as, "Ha Ha! You can't catch me!" but when you add sneaking and scouting, it gets as big as a full-scale multi-dimensional war of Capture the Flag.

Tag!

Tag, you're IT.
Tag, you're out.
Tag, you're in again.
Tag, I got what you were carrying.

Tag can be played in many forms, including lacrosse and football. The kids will show you how to play their tagging games.

You're Safe If You're Touching.

For example: Whoever is IT calls out, "You're safe if you are touching... a Cedar Tree, ...a sedimentary rock, ... fresh water, ... something red," then counts time, and goes chasing.

Everyone races to find a Cedar tree. Half of them get it wrong, which gives the chaser an advantage. Final advantage goes to those who know their nature names!

Proviso: Some children don't love sustained fast movement, so they sit out after a while. That's what's good about being put in jail by a tag.

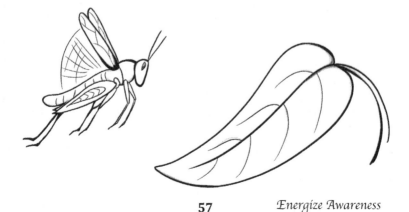

Energize Awareness

Awareness Games

Once their bodies are energized, you can slow down to play games that perk up their subtle sense of awareness, such as Hide and Sneak, Scout and Spy, Blindfold practice, and pop quizzes.

After a game is over, have a little debriefing chat about what they noticed, about sound and sight, about their own perceptive abilities.

Introducing Awareness

Teach about awareness. How the owl gazes widely then darts its eye to stare at the movement it notices in the grass; how deer turn their huge ears to capture the direction of sound; how raccoons feel their food underwater and blind moles smell theirs.

Practice doing that.

- **Do the owl-eye-wide-gaze** for a while. Where was your view brightest? What movement did you notice? What caught attention?
- **Make deer ears** and cup them back and forth. What do you hear, loud, soft, droning in the distance?
- **Feel your feet on the ground,** clothes on your body, temperature on your cheek. Where is the sun's heat coming from? How does the ground feel on your feet?
- **Kneel to touch the earth.** Dig in there. Smell it. Taste its chemistry with your fingertips.
- **Practice Cat Radar.** Move in shadows under cover, go still and watch, take off in new directions, follow what attracts you.

Invite stories of what they see and hear and smell and taste and touch.

Invite collective mapping of a territory they just walked through, noting what caught their sensory tendrils.

Do some research and regale them with tales of amazing animal feats of perception.

Give Pop Quizzes.
"Everybody close your eyes. Now, point to someone wearing white shoes. Point to East. Point to that loud crow caw."

Post questions on tree trunks, on sitting rocks, on porta-potty doors.

- Who has a black hood and a fan of white tail feathers?
- How do spiders build webs?
- When was this porta-potty last emptied?

By doing this, you are encouraging them to stay alert and aware of their surroundings. Kids will want to get the answers right, so they'll start widening their awareness too.

Hide and Sneak

Coyote's BEST game for reaching out with wild senses is Hide and Sneak. It's also the invisible entry to Sit Spot (see p. 77).

Hiding cover is a necessary bit of habitat for all animals. It is a private place, a little dark inside, where they can choose whether or not they want to be seen or disturbed. They wait in there, totally still, watching, hearing their own hearts beat.

Set the kids to hiding, seeking, and sneaking around, watchful and camouflaged while moving from place to place. Have some hide and others try to find them. Basically, set them to thinking like predator and prey.

Energize Awareness

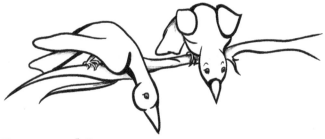

Scout and Spy

Coyote's other BEST game for honing those wild senses is Scout and Spy. It's the ultimate predator/prey game. It ups the ante.

By "Scout" Coyote means his kind of scouting, not so much with badges, but more like the scouts of the plains and mountains who explored slyly ahead of the people and read the signs.

They were spies, sneaking near the enemy fire circle, stealing horses, overhearing plans. They were providers, discovering the larders and hunting game.

In this activity, there are elements of stalking and hunting and elements of being caught. It's slightly competitive, the way predator/prey games ought to be, but it can be given nice soft edges and an elaborate winning system.

Scout and Spy games occur while traveling. A game can be a quick ambush along the trail. Or it can be a planned game. It can begin in storytelling and weave its tale.

Set the kids into teams that vie with each other. They lie in wait and ambush, they steal stuff and clip clothespins on each other, throw cones from behind trees, they capture flags. In doing these activities, they try to catch each other in failed awareness.

Maybe they build shelters, or carve secret hideaways, or construct forts.

Maybe they play fantasy war games. You can civilize them with rules and calibrations. It is always good to debrief events involving warfare in order to return to the trust and the peace.

Maybe in the end they reconcile and praise each other.

Any elaboration on **Capture the Flag** will do. Both teams protect their own flag while trying to capture the other's. Scouts get tagged, they go to jail, they get freed. All the while, they ambush and evade each other using sly movement, sharp senses, group strategy, and camouflage. Give teams goals, limits, challenges. You can also add in surprise obstacles.

Blindfold Classics

Temporarily blinding the eyes wakes up the other senses. It's very exciting!

Strap a cloth bandanna over our dominant visual antennae, and suddenly we feel the ground beneath our feet, hear every little thing, and reorient our balance in a different world.

Kids can get all antsy at the prospect of blindfolds.
Blindfolds can feel unhygienic and be scary and easy to cheat with, so go gently but firmly when you introduce the idea.

Bring clean, large-enough bandannas. Take some time to wrap heads to just the right tightness without catching up hair and glasses. Give them some time to acclimate to the strange feeling of being blind.

Centipede
Line up a few blindfolded kids with their hands on the shoulders of the person in front of them, then guide the train of kids along an irregular path.

Guided Walks
Pair two kids up, one seeing, one blind, and have them go on a walk. Go Meet a Tree and see if they can identify it afterwards with blindfold off. The guide learns about being trustworthy, and the guided learns to trust.

Follow a String
Mount a rope along a path, over and around obstacles, along sloping terrain. Have them follow it with their hands, sightlessly and soundlessly. This is great for balance, feeling their bodies, and hearing ahead and behind.

Drum Stalk

You can also send them off in a line at the low end of an open field and pound a drum, periodically, from the high end. The drum provides them with a guiding point to walk to with their vision removed. Watch as they stagger their way toward you in zigzags! Try moving the drum around.

Debrief

After these blinded experiences debrief as a group. Pull the kids in, release their eyes, and ask, "What was it like? How is it different now?" This is Coyote Magic!

Awestruck Moments

Sometimes eyes will be opened wide by an encounter with a dead seal or a caterpillar infestation or a landslide, things that strike down the heart. Other times you will meet a doe with her fawn, hold a firefly, witness an ethereal sunset, frolic in an inescapable downpour.

These are the wonderful, awesome moments. There is no activity for these serendipitous encounters. Only Coyote's yipping:

"Pay attention, Be astonished."

Stop everything and be here now!

Chapter 9

Forays

Children love ranging off into the great unknown. The 4 A's of such forays are Alive, Aware, Alert, and Active!

A foray is an adventure or expedition out into the field, beyond the game meadow, down the trails. Maybe it's a hike. Maybe an expedition.

Here the challenges begin. As the kids say, "the funnest part of all." Here be dragons.

Practice survival. If Energize Awareness was all about Predator and Prey, Forays are all about Survival, not only of self, but of community. Through Forays, together kids meet opportunities, crises, and challenges that are great for the collective soul. Coyote's favorite stuff!

With Forays, classroom teachers and mentors in recreational programs can find their heyday. You can make serious science projects and summer adventures out of these Forays.

Errands

However, the very first Foray is a simple matter.

Errand Commands
- Go pick berries.
- Find me something that looks like this.
- Help make camp.
- Go together and build a shelter.
- Bring me a Band-Aid!

Every group has kids operating at different speeds and styles. When most are engaged, but some are errant, it is time to give the errant errands.

Errands are usually for individuals. Watch, and when the time is right, pick out individuals to send on small personal missions. When they need a task, a break, a lift, or an advanced project.

If the dog brings the ball back to your feet, the best training reward is attention. So pay attention and enjoy their stories when they return from errands.

Tracking

Tracking is Coyote's BEST foray for The Art of Questioning.

Detective Work. Tracking is a metaphor for focused inquiry, for detective work. An animal leaves tracks in the mud and many other signs as well – like leaf chews, tree scratches, scats and scrapes, worn little trails, dens, lays, tunnels, holes, dirt kicked up, etchings under bark. These are all clues to its mysterious story, and they make the invisible visible.

Plan on taking lots of time along the way for curiosity – about tracks, about plants, about nests, about anything and everything!

Coyote tracks. It's a key to his character. Tracking means sticking your nose to the dirt and following clues to wherever they take you. It's an intense focus on some aspect.

You can track actual footprints, but also you can track distance and elevation gain. You can track how the dirt beneath your feet changes in rock texture. You can track garden growth. You can track your expenses, your mileage, your calories.

If you watch through seasons,
- You can track how plants grow – from spring's glowing greens to fall's leaves in the wind.
- You can track incidence and quantity of bird species at various times of year.
- You can track climate changes.
- You can monitor water quality.
- You can foresee weather trends.

These are all great school science projects.

Animal Tracking. Best of all, you can track animal footprints. If you live near sand or mud, or if you live in thick forest duff, this is really exciting because when you find a track, you realize the wild animal was right here.

What kind of an animal was it? Was it passing through, hunkered down, sleeping, nibbling, suddenly turning?

Take a field guide for mammals and mammal tracks of your area and you can figure out:

- » **Who** – *identification* – Who left this track? Ask questions about size, shape, number of toes, claw marks, heel pads, tail drags.
- » **What** – *interpretation* – What direction is it going? What gait? Was it turning, stopping, jumping?
- » **When** – *aging* – When did it pass this way? Study effects of drying out, rain drops, wind, falling debris.
- » **Where** – *trailing* – Where is it right now? Where is the next print or sign? Follow it.
- » **Why** – *ecological* – Look at the bigger picture of what you know is going on, to understand why it is here – food sources, water, shelter.
- » **How** – *empathy* – Imagine being the animal. What was it thinking? Was it hungry, thirsty, hot or cold?

Tracking and Questioning go hand in hand. It's the perfect way for YOU to practice Not Answering. It's pointing them to follow clues and solve problems.

Mystery Stations are great training for this questioning attitude. Experts among you facilitate a set of stations, and mentor newcomers into looking closely at evidence. Then together they pool their knowledge to come to conclusions to answer questions such as, "Who left that track?"

Track-infested Trails also work, but take more preparation. You drag a stick with a plow point to leave a trail, or hang pink flags, or strew litter, or stow prizes in knotholes. Then they track the trail.

Knowing Plants by Name

More casual and ubiquitous are encounters with low-lying vegetation, flowering or edible plants, thorned or berry bushes, things chewing holes in leaves or weaving cocoons underneath them.

Plants are the baseline of all land travel. Wandering among plants in the understory, you can nibble on edible leaves and berries, find shelter for nasty weather, or just plain poke around, sniffing.

Tear a big leaf into five pieces and get the kids to piece it together as a jigsaw puzzle. They notice veins and watery edges.

Show the difference between edible plants and their poisonous lookalikes.

Gather a salad of petals and leaves.

Make a poultice of a plant that cures the sting of a nearby poisonous one.

Play Plant Identification routinely. You collect eight leaves that grow nearby, they get a quick glimpse of them laid out on a handkerchief, they run off hunting. Each group or individual wins who returns with a leaf identical to one of the eight you collected. Repeat to remember.

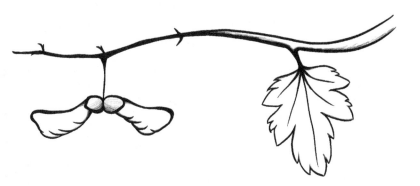

Adventures and Hunts

These are the height of focused attention.

Adventures
Ad + venture means, "flow toward." Use Cat Radar to range out into the unknown toward a point of fascination.

Go on a night walk, ford a river, catch a fish, camp overnight, swim in a swamp, build a tree house!

Adventure is often unplanned as well, like getting a little lost, or caught in the rain, or visited by a hawk, or called to climb a tree. Let adventure announce itself and then jump into it! Safely, of course.

Scavenger Hunts
Scavenger suggests tasty tidbits out there (if you like dead things) but to find them, you have to fly in circles looking with vulture eyes.

Provide a list of things to hunt for. Set out an individual challenge or groups can compete in a time limit.

- Could be "Find things in these five colors"
- Could be bring back three kinds of wood for a fire
- Could be a bird list
- Could be rarities that will take all day to see – a hawk, a volcanic rock, a bird's breast feather

Review the accuracy of their finds. Make it a competition, or not.

Create a Treasure Hunt map of your territory with challenges to navigate. Bury a treasure somewhere on it.

Create a list of serial clues, maybe in rhyme or riddle, then plant each clue along the way. They follow the clues, leaving them in place, leading the kids toward the buried treasure. (With these activities, you do have to plan ahead.)

Geocaching offers a fun techy twist to this. Send them off with devices to find GPS coordinates where treasure is hidden. Sign in, take something, leave something.

Fantasy Hunts

Children love a mythological storyline, so take them on snipe hunts, seeking Sasquatch. Plant dinosaur tracks and have them find all kinds of dinosaur evidence along the way.

Put on costumes and play Robin Hood or Harry Potter. Station imaginary persons from your Village along the trail one day to surprise them. Wear invisibility cloaks. Engage the children's current fantasies, but tweak the setting.

Explorations and Expeditions

These both begin with Ex, which means "out." To ex-plore is to follow what cries to be discovered. To ex-ped is to do it on foot. Think Lewis and Clark or Mount Everest or the North Pole.

These require planning and gear and usually involve drawing maps and collecting samples in jars.

Older children love expeditions that challenge endurance and intellect. The more epic the better. Make a big deal out of an upcoming long expedition. Give it a purpose: to collect, to explore, to map. Make a list and gather gear for it. Train for it. Manage it for risk.

Classrooms can develop units that are extended explorations. Set up a mural along an entire wall of your classroom, and fill it in over the year. Collect impressive data. Include parents and experts. Make your finale a two-day bioblitz. Present your findings to the national archives or simply to their parents.

Survival Practice

Practicing Survival is the ultimate 4-A – Alive, Aware, Alert, and Active. It begins with the story of those who live off the land, without the grid to give them light, heat, food, shelter, and direction.

So, find your way to tell that story. Read *The Tracker* by Tom Brown Jr., or see a survival show. Tell your own story of camping out, hiking the Pacific Crest Trail, eating wild edible plants.

Then set up a survival practice journey that is guaranteed to provide a memorable experience of thrival, which is a mix of both surviving and thriving. Adapt the journey to age and group and place. Some possibilities include:

- Go out at dawn.
- Travel in the dark.
- Camp out.
- Make a fire, keep it going.
- Eat wild plants. Starve if you can't find them.
- Kill and consume all parts of an animal.
- Build a shelter and live in it.
- Go out Solo for a while.

Chapter 10

Wandering

Children love hanging out without grownups interfering. When just out-of-sight of the supervisors, they have explored their independent learning curves since the beginning of time.

Wandering is a relaxation of focus. No agenda. No destination. No timeline. After hard play, structure collapses, and they can do their own thing on their own time.

Take a Break!

Children need down time. A break provides a time for taking care of snacks and water and bunched up socks, for the private ones to get away from too many people, for the passionate ones to pursue their craft, for the chatty ones to talk about whatever they want.

This is a really challenging activity element for educators of large groups in a hurry. But it is SO important. We all know the regenerating impact of breaking focus and napping!

This is free time for the Coyote Mentor to circle around in the background cover as the kids navigate their social worlds, watching for clues about how to lure the group from here on.

Make time for Unstructured Time.
- Stop for rest and water
- Stretch out and nap
- Simply play
- Chat idly
- Finish up what you want to

Wander Off!

Unstructured time can be a Wander off the beaten track, time spent just poking around, or when you are drawn by a serendipitous attraction.

> "Hey, there's a bush full of ripe berries!"
> "Hey, let's climb to that outcropping of rock on the hillside with the sun on it!"
> "Hey, check out these tracks in the floodwater mud."

Wandering is a time of going off-leash, off path, but under voice command, meaning they aren't to go too far from the group. It can be:

- Bushwhacking off-trail
- Gathering resources, berries, wood
- Darting off to dunk in cool water

Learn to navigate. Sometimes a Wander can get you lost. Learn some skills for bushwhacking and finding your way back.

- Leaving markers by the trail
- Sight-lining from one high point to another
- Using map and compass
- Making contact

If you are lost,

> Stand still
> The forest knows
> Where you are.
> You must let it find you.
>   – David Wagoner

Chapter 11
Show & Tell

Children love telling the Story of their Day. This is not "storytelling" where YOU do a dramatic rendition, but instead "show and tell" BY THE KIDS. When they share little tidbits of the day that are fresh and full of information.

Toward the end of your outing, it's time for kids to act like scouts returning to the campfire at Home Base in the Village, telling of discoveries, amazements, disappointments, funny things, what they learned, what they found, where they went.

Story Circle

Routinely end with Story Circle, a place set up for showing and telling. Circle up, quiet down, and listen to each other's stories.

Maybe do it by passing a "talking stick" around a circle with silence and attentiveness surrounding the child about to speak, and no interruptions.

Maybe do it as a show and tell examination, with each presentation of a Find putting the finder on the hot seat. Who, what, when, where, why?

Maybe do it as a group story where all chime in or act out.

Story Circle can be fast or slow, depending on your situation.

> Coyote's job is to bait the hook, tease
> the fish, snag a bite, bring it in.

Capturing Stories
Catch their stories by throwing out good questions.

> » What were our high points?
> » What obstacles did we meet?
> » How did we work together?
> » What was the scariest part?
> » What was funny?
> » What brought you to your knees?
> » What made your heart sing?
> » What did you discover about yourself?
> » What did you learn about nature?
> » What do you want to do next?

Get them started, and then it's time for Coyote to knead his bed and lie down, while he listens sharply, and yips in with perky comments and questions.

- What did that look like, exactly?
- Where were you, exactly?

Story Groupings
If you have too many for a story circle, break them into pairs or smaller circles, so everyone gets a chance to say their words.

Showing Finds

Having a prop to show makes it less daunting when children look out and discover they have an audience.

At Show and Tell, everyone gathers around the Find – a flower, a cocoon, a bone, a geode – and shows interest in it. It's like being gently showered with appreciation.

At Home Base, have some nature tables set up, a big one with guides and tools and specimens, and some little ones where Finds can be placed lovingly as museum pieces, or little treasures on an altar.

Upon gathering up for Story Circle, let the finds be nearby for use as needed. Call on kids who have something to show, and coax the story out of them with questions.

Invite examination. Look at mosses and leaves, moths and feathers, with magnifying lenses. Find them in field guides. Have bright ideas about what they are.

Finds can accumulate into science projects and museum shows.

Mapping

Develop a beautiful map of your world. You can do Story of the Day by circling up around a big blank paper and drawing highlights onto the group's ongoing map.

Start with drawing a sketch of your territory. Use pencil and have an eraser on hand. Show North. Show Home Base. Show trails. Draw boundaries. Name landmarks. Once your territory is generally mapped, you can go over it with pen to make the staple elements permanent.

Show & Tell

The question is, "Where did we go today?" "What did we see?" "Did we all see the same thing but from a different angle?" Debate, then draw these highlights on the map. Ongoing programs develop mountable maps!

No Paper? Just draw your map with a stick in the dirt or a finger in the sand.

Real maps, either of roads or contour lines, are a great learning tool. You can't get some kids' heads out of them.

Drawing a map puts all that sensory information into a spatial and logical part of the brain. Great for getting a group to cooperate actively like officers in the control room.

Challenge them all to keep a little notebook that holds some hand-drawn maps.

Maybe they'd like to create their own fantasy world with a full blown fantastic map.

Field Guides

Field guides are wonderful children's books.

They are written for grownups, but full of pictures and captions that kids love. They impress images, tell nature stories, and are the textbook for nature literacy.

Notice that some field guides have photos, and some have drawings. The photos are closer to the truth, but drawings highlight field marks. All have introductions to how they work, with nice pages of structural hints. The Golden Guide series are terrific for kids, but they miss your rarer local species.

Online resources abound. There are identification keys to most things, including bird songs. Phone apps can identify a bird song just by holding the phone up toward the song or draw lines between stars to show constellations in a night sky.

Appreciate the centuries of quiet watchful hours exploring, observing, and species-naming that our forebears have put into making these field guides. Tell heroic stories about the authors and artists. Go visit a nature photo gallery. Watch documentaries. Imagine getting a job doing that!

How to Browse a Field Guide
It is all about asking questions and using your detective skills until you find the perfect match.

"What did you find?"

> "Ah, a cone!" "Ooh, a bone!"

"What did you see?"

> "Ah, a red headed bird."

- Let's see if we can find a picture of that in here. Which book do we need?

- It's kind of like that, but not quite. Let's look more closely.

- Ah, it's got to be one of those three. Which one is it?

- Where did you find it? When? Let's see if it's in our range map for right here.

- Did you hear its call? Let's play this sound from our bird call app.

- Hey, check that out (that has nothing to do with what we're looking for). Isn't that a cool picture? Let's look for one of those!

Use field guides to spark questions for Story of the Day. Elaborate the story with details and specifics from their field guide research.

Chapter 12
Still, Quiet, Alone

Children love belonging in the wild world. The best way to fit in is to be still, quiet, alone, and often, in a safe place outside.

Sit Spot is the core of the Core Routines of Nature Connection. In the midst of our constant activity, it is an In-Activity, a meditation with mind still, letting the senses open to the natural world, becoming familiar with the wild.

By calling this segment of the Flow of Activities "Still, Quiet, and Alone," we expand the notion of Sit Spot to include some quiet activities that serve to enhance that familiarity.

Drawing, writing, examining, planting and cultivating, fishing and hunting, processing, weaving, or carving, even hiking and paddling – all have the effect of Sit Spot: times when you are mentally still, letting your senses open to the world around you.

Sit Spot In-Activities

Create ways to sit outdoors
- Still
- Quiet
- Alone
- In the same place
- Often

But, falling short of aim, look for opportunities to enable children to be slightly alone outdoors sometimes.

Once you quiet down, the animals come looking at you. You look back. You watch their daily rituals; the signs they leave. The signs of your inside world become increasingly invisible.

When you go to the same place repeatedly, the wild animals come closer. They begin to talk with you. You feel like you belong here.

Over time, it becomes an intimate experience, a sense of being in friendly and wise company out there alone in the woods. The spirits of things vibrate with messages. You get a dreamy feeling of being at home outdoors.

Coyote visits Sit Spots.

Hide and Seek is the portal. Children don't love sitting still outdoors. It's very awkward for kids who just like doing things and it can be frightening all alone.

So, Coyote's trick entry to Sit Spot is to play any version of Hide and Seek. Make it hard for the Seekers to find the Hiders so they have to sit there a long, long time, waiting quietly, alone with the

Still, Quiet, Alone

cobwebs and beetles. They think they're just playing a game, but really, they're learning Sit Spot.

Solo
Discern when the time is right, then set them out in private places to sit for a period of time. Maybe they can write or draw or use magnifying lenses.

- Spread them one by one along a trail, to be observant for 5 minutes;
- Or each pick a spot on the edge of your Home Base to visit every day for a feasible duration;
- Or assign them to go to a place they like in the school-yard or at home and schedule it into the homework regime.

Listening for Bird Language
Sit Spot means still and quiet, which makes you invisible. First the body gets settled, then the thumping heart calms, the legs adjust, breathing slows. As you become still, life begins around you again. You begin to hear the birds chatting with the other creatures nearby.

What perks up then is hearing what's out there and the rustle of weather. You pay attention to alarm calls, insect buzz, and raindrops landing on leaves. You quiet down to listen. Wildlife turns its ears away from you.

You begin to hear your own voices, of chatter, and willing attention, of thanking, or caring. You feel things through. You get a sense of direction. You return peaceful to your group.

Debriefing
Gather together and share stories of what happened in their hiding places and Sit Spots.

- What did they see, hear, smell, touch?
- What happened?
- What did they remember?
- What did they realize?
- What did they love?

Imagining

Sit Spot is where images imprint. The spiral of a leaf, the color of a bird's eyebrow, the gait of your dog. Sit Spot is a good time to get private and delve into sensory imagination. It's a time to discern in quiet awareness, feeling and smelling, noticing patterns.

Sensory "search images," were the vocabulary of preliterate hunters and gatherers. Hunters use them to zone into telltale signs of quarry. Wildlife biologists use them to spot things on the move.

An image starts with excited focus:
- Wow!! Big bird on the wing!
- What did it look like?
- Can you draw it? Give it words?
- Let's find it here in this field guide. What did the underside of its wingtip look like?

An image digests into memory at Sit Spot.
Imprint images of the day by remembering them, looking into them, taking them in hand and looking closely, drawing them, or writing about them, preparing to notice them again.

The richer in multi-sensory input the image is, the wider its storage space is textured throughout the brain.

Magnifying

Get close enough to be stunned.

Teach the use of magnifying lenses to enlarge hidden worlds in nature. Acquire a set of child-handy jeweler's loupes that they can make work, and teach them to magnify.

Start with seeing their fingerprints, the hairs on their arms. Then get a private eye on grains of sand in rock, veins and fur on leaves, civilizations and drainage systems in moss!

Invent worlds to scale. Take one square foot of your landscape. Pretend it's a whole world. Give it avatars, little people, waterfalls and talking trees. Involve kids' current fantasy characters but tweak the setting.

Fantasize about living in tiny natural worlds!
But, instead of anthropomorphizing (imagining the tree is like you), imagine you are alive like the tree, standing in one place for hundreds of years, photosynthesizing and drinking water through mycorrhizal roots.

Look closely, and engage their minds with questions.

> » What does it remind you of?
>
> » What else? What else?
>
> » Why, what do those two things have in common?
>
> » Why is it built like that – what are those parts for?
>
> » What if it were bigger, smaller, harder? What would it be like then?
>
> » Could you use this idea to design something useful (Bio-mimicry engineering)?

Sketching

Pull out a pencil and pad and draw what you're looking at. Choose your subject: a picked flower, a sunbathing turtle, a tall tree, a shoreline or a picture from a field guide.

Method
- Look close and long at the subject.
- Then turn your eyes away to the sketchpad.
- Draw from memory.
- Then look back. Check the details you weren't sure about against your sketch.
- Correct connections and proportions.
- Do this back and forth.
- Develop it into more than a sketch.

Sketching Ideas

- **Line sketch:** An outline or a stick drawing that captures the shape and structure.
- **Spirit Sketch:** A few lines that capture the gist of the attitude, including head turns, postures, movement, branching habit, budding expression.
- **Wrapper sketch:** Lots of shading, fur and feather and veins, that records the texture of the outer costume.
- **Bits and pieces of botany:** Include stem, leaves, and flower parts, labeled.

Journaling

Journaling is a routine that stretches and etches all the images a little further into heart and mind. It turns experience into thoughts and words.

Get kids to have fun with words. Find five words for "green" and pick the most fitting. Give that bug a name. Find language for that weird smell. Describe "awesome" without saying "awesome."

As appetizers for writing in journals, team up to fit stories into little poem forms like the seventeen syllabled haiku or the rhythm of a marching song. Invent puns and riddles and limericks while you're going along. (Perfect for long rides in the car).

Start it up deliberately. Hand out notebooks, and pens. "Write your name on yours." If they don't yet know how to write, provide a scribe.

Teach some daily headings, designate a short writing period, provide a topic, and get together at the end to coordinate findings, tell what you wrote.

Make a regular practice of it, until the stories begin to add up, until some journals want to become private, and some turn into great nature writing. Just do it, keep a journal, until it becomes a habit some kids can't live without.

Fill in a Field Inventory
Here's a staple of Coyote Mentoring. Keep a Field Inventory. Copy this list with space between items. Every day, fill spaces in with notes on any magic moments that fit under the headings. Every week put it together and hand it in. Try to fill all the spaces.

- **Earth:** rocks and soils and their beings
- **Waters:** in all their forms
- **Low-lying plants:** growth style, location, abundance
- **Animals:** big and small, sight and sign
- **Trees:** height, shape, movement
- **Birds:** everywhere in song and flight
- **Weather:** wind, clouds, storms
- **Sun:** light, heat, time of day
- **Moon:** in all phases
- **Stars:** in their swirling constellations

Bypass writing frustration by offering help with writing and a butterfly net full of tips and allowances. Journaling is a private thing designed to evoke delightful mind's eye imagination. Let it not be a chore. Or if they love to write, then by all means, keep a fat diary of stories, poetry, and narrative.

Taming and Tending

Taming as love. The tide turns when children know their home and feel they belong in the natural community.

Love is a taming process. To the birds, a band of children yelling into the woods is wild, just as the birds are "wildlife" to the children.

To make friends with wild things is beautifully illustrated in Saint Exupery's book, *Little Prince*. A young prince of a very small planet finds himself tamed by a fox he visits, a sheep he tends, and a rose he loves.

He waits for the fox tenderly, and the fox instructs him on how to approach, how to be there routinely, how to come closer each time.

The taming, of course, is mutual. They become friends, so they watch out for each other and depend on each other and tend to each other gladly.

The fox represents Sit Spot.

Tending as Kinship

The notion of Sit Spot, a place you know intimately from frequent visits, can expand to include a restoration site, where you pull things out, plant things in with little flags, then return to prune the recovery.

It can be a garden, a vacant lot, or a school plot – where you prepare the soil, sow the seeds, water, watch, and harvest.

Tending as Kinship can also be:

> » Training the puppy – feeding, cleaning up after, walking, teaching to obey commands.
> » Keeping up an annual monitor of weather patterns, harvest times, spring ice breakup.
> » Mowing, pruning, tearing down, building trail – big heavy work, very satisfying if done for fun.
> » Raising animals for food and market.
> » Creating a Home Base campsite. Sleeping there. Inviting friends. Starting a nature school.
> » Tending a wildlife shelter. Releasing healed birds and watching them fly off.

Chapter 13

Ceremony

Children love Ceremony and remember it fondly.

Nature Connection brings up awe and reverence, sorrow, companionship, compassion, courage, transformation. These things call for spiritual recognition.

Ceremony honors a deeper level of being than play. When children are prepared for ceremony, they get very wide-eyed and hushed. If they will be singled out for honors, they glow and shiver with anticipation. If there are guests and gifts and dress-up and celebrations following, kids will remember ceremony as turning points.

Mentor steps in strongly for ceremony. Gandalf sheds his disguise and arrives dazzling with staff ablaze.

Openings and Closings

Opening and closings signify thresholds of ceremonial space. There is a moment of silence, a hush. A hand over the heart, a bow and shanti. Begin ceremony with thanksgiving and inclusion. Close gatherings with separation and blessings for safe journeys onward.

Here you are, starting up your planned outing. Everything is a scramble – cars, kids, equipment, forms. So many dramas have already occurred – over breakfast, fourth period, the road trip.

Take a deep breath, quiet down and be present. Just be quiet for a count of seconds. Send thanks and love and prayers and blessings and requests out into the world.

Circle Up the kids. Make a fire in the middle of your gathering – sing a song, light a candle, throw down a gauntlet. Deliver a priestly moment of thanksgiving. Be a little stunning. Use your best words. Help your wards be insightfully hopeful.

Here you are, at the end of an outing, so much has happened. Take a deep breath. Find your own center. Grab the tiller.

Circle up the kids and help them be insightfully thankful before you send them back into the scurry.

Honor Rites of Passage

Rites of Passage ceremonies offer ways to reflect on and digest experience. Take time to celebrate transitions like challenges met, bonds forged, birthdays, and graduations. Acknowledge accomplishments achieved with certification or proficiency or mastery or honorable mention!

Prepare an event. Announce it and invite their families and mentors as witnesses. Prepare costumes and props for it. Plan to highlight individual and group transitions by telling the story in your finest words. Invite valedictorians from the class. Prepare little gifts, bestow new names.

Ceremonially single out individuals who have achieved some stage or standard. Name their names, explain their accomplishments, give them a badge of honor. Enable intimate moments and private congratulations.

Celebrate with friends and family, letting the honored individuals be the stars of attention among mentors.

Gifting

The giving of gifts is a fundamental ceremony that fits many occasions whether it be a greeting gift, a potluck party, a wopila, a rendezvous trade fest, or just hanging a memory in a tree.

It is a ritual in many cultures to think about, gather, shape, wrap, and present a Gift. It involves leavening a swell of generosity.

If your program lasts over time, if it has a Home Base and Village time, then you are set up for making crafts as giveaways.

Kids will want to busy their hands making their finds into necklaces and hanging chimes, weaving baskets out of willow and nettle, carving utensils, burnishing walking sticks, cooking berry pies.

Focus this crafting into a ceremonial plan and create an event for the presentation of giveaways.

It may be taking a little biodegradable doodad to hang in Sit Spot, or leaving a circle of stones there. It may be spreading out a trade blanket and piling it with homemade things to barter or give outright to visitors. It could be a feast.

Make ceremonial space to savor the giving and receiving, to appreciate what went into the gifts, how they are given, and what they signify.

Seasonal Celebrations

Create holidays based on natural events. Solstices and Equinoxes, eclipses, full moons, the arrival of monsoons. The annual inundation of the marshes. The cracking up of river ice in Alaska. The return of the swallows to Capistrano.

Go to a place for this. Climb a mountain at Easter or take blankets to a night meadow under a meteor shower. Wear warm boots and wait for the dusk arrival of the trumpeter swans. Go out into the storm and climb a tree waving in the wind like John Muir.

Celebrate the four seasonal turning dates, the equinoxes and solstices that mark the beginning of spring, summer, fall, and winter.

Clean out and refresh the nature table. Decorate Home Base with the flags of the season.

Hold a ceremony with a talking stick to reflect on how our human lives are pressured and challenged and changed with every turning season.

What is the Story of the Season?

What do we look forward to eagerly?

What are our intentions?

Follow up with a party. Coyote insists! Any way you can. Eat, Howl, Yip.

SECTION 4
Creating Your Program

Imagine what YOUR Invisible School will look like!

Design YOUR program to fit your Site and Situation and adapt it to align with the Flow of Activities and sync with the Natural Cycle.

Chapter 14
One Size Fits All?

——— 🐾 🐾 ———

We've addressed a wide spectrum of people, operating in a wide range of habitat, as if One Size Fits All. We all know that isn't true, that scale matters, and so does age and place and type of kids and styles of mentors.

Your program can be as simple as walking the dog, and as complex as a month-long camping hike or a classroom science unit.

Everybody is different, in different places, with different clientele and different goals, but Coyote has a plan.

Your Site

Ask yourself, "What's My Site?" How wild, how accessible, how challenging is my landscape, my hazards, my climate?

Wherever you are – in your place, your weather, your bugs, your common plants – this is your Book of Nature, and we can't address it specifically in this pocket guide.

You may be only one field-guide-step ahead of the kids in knowing names of wild things, but you are the expert, the nature lover, here in your place.

We know that because you are reading our book to this point.

If you want your kids to love what you love about your wild world, look at your place with animal eyes.

Where would be good spots for Home Base? Where could you wander? What calls for exploration?

Every activity needs to be adapted to place. Hide and Seek works great in the woods, but what about the desert? Tracking is easy in sand, but what about forest debris?

Only you know! Mine the Activities you just read for ones that will work in your scenario. Adapt them to your site and find ways to make them your own.

Your Situation

Next ask, **"What's My Situation?"** What do you want to do with your clientele outdoors? Who are your kids? How old, how eager, how abled, how many?

Here are your Situations, as we said in the beginning:

Families
Parents with children of all ages who want
to explore, hike, camp, or just hang out in the
outback with neighbors.

Teachers
Instructors, mentors, coaches, tutors who have
the opportunity to get students outdoors.

Outdoor Guides
You plan and guide seasonal outdoor programs.

Every one of you can make these activities work for your people. Begin by knowing your students well. Where are they on the developmental spectrum? What gifts and stumbling blocks do they present? What are your educational parameters and how can you guide this flock to meet goals?

Set up Home Base, agreements, limits and challenges suitable to the ones you're with.

One Size Fits All?

It helps to harness your program to some Core Routines. Institute a learning culture that practices habits of Sit Spot, Story of the Day, and the best of the eleven other Core Routines.

Bring on Coyote and Mentor, getting in touch with those two parts of yourself. Then let them design through you. Start with where your students are at. Make a schedule with a flow of activities (see The Flowing Activities, p. 96 and following). Set out and then make changes as needed.

Team Teaching

It takes a Village. When Coyote Mentoring, the art and science, is applied with serious intention, you need other grownups to bounce off ideas with.

The kids, too, need more than one mentor to spot their genius, have private talks with, promote curiosity, and provide particular expertise.

If you want to do Coyote Mentoring satisfyingly, it really, really helps to have about two mentors for every 10-16 kids, to teach in a team. If you are taking just your children out, then it is possible to do it alone.

Seriously, when you go out in nature with kids, it's always good to have two adults, or one adult and a competent grown-up youth, to handle emergencies.

Recruiting a Team
Bring in parents, neighbors, grandparents, aunties, uncles, apprentices, volunteers, local naturalists, neighborhood seniors, expert guests, and capable teens. Best of all, get a buddy to do this with you.

Training a team
- If you've recruited naturalists, train them to mentor.
- If you've recruited parents, train them to step out of their parent box into Coyote Mentoring.
- If you've recruited teachers, teach them the 50-50 Principle!

Consider applying the roles of the Natural Cycle (see next chapter) to tasks your team members carry.

- **East** handles people issues: registration, sign-in, welcoming, caregiver relations, welcoming and inspiring.
- **South** handles site issues, arrangements, equipment, risk management.
- **West** handles program design and leads teaching.
- **North** produces the program and oversees them all.

Be prepared for skirmishes among adults. The old adage – "forming, storming, norming, performing" generally holds true for teaching teams.

Planning and Debriefing
Try to get leaders together early, before kids arrive, to review the plan and prepare the possibilities.

When it's over, take time for the team to do your own Thanksgiving Address and tell your own Stories of the Day. When the commitment is over, celebrate your collaboration.

Natural Grouping

Coyote Mentors range from grandparents with a kid and a dog after school, to classroom teachers with 5 classes of 30 in the winter in Manitoba.

Most of you are in the middle – working with groups of reasonable size in fair weather.

If your group is bigger than 12, you'll want to subdivide it into smaller units for some activities.

Here is advice about how to manage subdivision so kids get variety in who they are with and some moderately supervised time to learn on their own.

Grouping
When you need to break into small groups, here are classic forms:

- **Buddies:** pairs who account for each other's whereabouts, go on errands together.
- **Teams:** small groups that work as homerooms or hoods, they get to know each other well. They give themselves nature-gangsta names. "Hungry Badgers!"
- **Chore Squads:** small teams designated to tend to logistics of all kinds – gathering firewood, leading thanksgiving. They salute to orders.
- **Interest Groups:** The scientists, trackers, fire starters, harvesters, cooks, artists, gamers, study-groupers - whatever little guilds emerge. They conspire and collaborate on expeditions and projects. Set these on tasks and plan time for their work.

Subdividing
You may wish to make designer groups. Assess how individuals will best fit in a small self-managing group and designate its members. You may want to balance ages and genders. You may want to aggregate friends and separate contentious pairs. If so, it is fun to plan up teams, as coaches do over midnight oil, and then announce names of kids in each group.

But if random grouping is all you need, here is a timeworn technique for subdivision.

Simply Count off: 1,2,3,4 as you point at each child. Remember your number. Go meet each other in your number groups.

Then send groups off as teams, with instructions, on errands, or to stations.

Re-gather and debrief in a circle allowing all to hear the story by a representative from each group.

Chapter 15
Natural Cycle

Coyote Mentoring proposes a scheme for designing the flow of your program that seems to work pretty well for nearly everyone. Our lineage calls it Eight Shields.

In this book, we'll call our simple version the Natural Cycle.

Imagine a band of birdsong from pole to pole, bursting into a dawn chorus as the earth turns steadily eastward into sunrise.

Now imagine standing in a spot outdoors for a day as the earth twirls slowly onward from the dawn chorus to hot noon to cool evening to dark night. Watch the arc of the sun.

As the earth spins daily into the sun and away, and as it turns yearly on its oval-tipped orbit, it leans us into daily and seasonal moods, changes the way our weathers and energies feel.

This is the flow of the Natural Cycle. We all know it in our bones. Doesn't it make sense to design your program to follow this universal flow of energies?

In his book, *Sharing the Joy of Nature with Children*, Joseph Cornel, father of the idea of Flow Learning, suggests that outdoor programs begin, as do morning and spring, with excitement.

Then use that energy to focus, then relax and deepen into connection, just as the day and the seasons turn.

We agree, and have organized our Flowing Activities section to follow the energies of the sun around the earth, from sunrise to the next dawn gleaming into the deep of night.

The Flowing Activities

	Activity	Season	Time	Mood
East	Greet & Gather	Spring	Sunrise	Inspiring
SE	Energize Awareness		Morning	Motivating
South	Foray	Summer	Midday	Focusing
SW	Wander		Afternoon	Relaxing
West	Show & Tell	Fall	Sunset	Congregating
NW	Still, Quiet, Alone		Dusk	Reflecting
North	Ceremony	Winter	Midnight	Integrating
NE	Home Base		Dawn	Regenerating

Program Design

The first thing you do in planning your program is design the Program itself. This is a series of activities that you will run your people through in a given period of time to form a tidy learning unit with beginning, middle, and measurable outcome.

If it's a simple one-time outing, it's a Lesson Plan.

If it's a series of lesson plans, it's a Course.

If it's a group of courses, it's a Curriculum.

So ask yourself, what are you designing?

Identify the goals and objectives you have for your program. Do you just want to have fun? Do you want to teach something specific? Do you want to build a learning community over time? What's your time frame?

If you just want to have fun connecting kids invisibly with Nature, make a Lesson Plan for your outing. Simply pick out a few suggestions from the Flowing Activities section that will fit in your time frame, and string them together in a natural flow in the time you have.

You'll likely hit and miss getting the timing right, so simply revise for next time. Remember to plan time for to Tell a Story to get things started. Make a moment for Wandering and for Sitting Still.

For fun, try to run fast through the whole Natural Cycle when you're just taking your grandchild out for a walk with the dog. Or just do two directions – Foray (South) and Show and Tell (West).

If you want to teach Nature Literacy, you can do this through a Course in wildcraft or mapping or monitoring or journaling or tracking or using field guides or learning a survival skill or craft. Whatever you choose, make that focus your Main Event (your Foray) and design around it. Even with such a goal, always start with Greeting and Gathering, take a break when needed, and end with Show and Tell.

If you want to build a learning community, design a Curriculum where the same group meets repeatedly over time. Focus on teaching and instilling the Core Routines. Do this until they become regular practices during your time together, so all you need to do is cue them.

> *"Go to your Sit Spot. Take an hour to research Field Guides. Teams, fill in your Maps. Group, Listen to that Bird Language!"*

Design a curriculum that goes round and round the Natural Cycle, so learners accumulate knowledge and hone skills incrementally. Measure outcomes at the end; they might be stunning.

Pay special attention to coaching your community to work together peacefully and with uplifted bright minds, greeting newness with curiosity, and leaving things better than they found them. Start and end with an effort at ceremony.

The Scheme

Allow the Natural Cycle to govern the flow of your program design, because it makes energetic sense.

Design your program to follow this sequence:

1. **NE:** Start at your Home Base, this is the place you create to begin and end each gathering.

2. **E:** Call the circle to Greet and Gather, getting to know each other, sharing hopes and fears, and appreciations.

3. **SE:** Get moving and Energize Awareness with warm-up activities, run, race, and tag, hide and sneak.

4. **S:** Embark on a major focused Foray somewhere outdoors. This can be a hike, an expedition, an adventure, a project, a study, a challenge, or maybe an all-day game of Capture the Flag. Practice all the Core Routines you can – use your senses deliberately, imagine being wild animals, question, track, map, develop images, become nature literate one happenchance accumulation at a time.

5. **SW:** Allow focus to Wander. Take a break. Let individual curiosity lead.

6. **W:** Circle up again for Show and Tell. Pass the talking stick around so everyone gets a turn. Tell stories, share finds, map routes, and recall magic moments together.

7. **NW:** Find time to be Sit Still, Quiet, & Alone. Journal, listen to Bird Language, simply be alone in nature.

8. **N:** End with ceremonial appreciation at Home Base (NE).

Interruptions in Travel

"Interruptions in travel are dancing lessons from God."

You have a tidy plan, you're in the middle of a focused expedition, but the kids find a beautiful dead owl.

Awe and grief descend powerfully upon the group. You look at it lovingly, touch its talons, carefully spread it to a full wingspan. Gross things are eating its rotting flesh. Tender emotions prevail.

So, don't jump back into your plan. Instead, ask yourself, "Where are we on the cycle?" The winter night of North, in the flow of Ceremony, Sit Spot, Home Base. The place of awe and grief, of going inward and feeling deeply. Invite private sitting, quiet group reflections, maybe tell a story to make meaning of the event.

Then, when the energies are ready, do a gathering game more communal than originally planned, and then do something energetic and attentive, so you meld your group again and restore excitement.

Now you're back on cycle.

Circle back to your original focus before the wondrous interruption.

East

Activity: Greet & Gather

Natural Cycle: Sunrise/Spring
*Dawn tenderness and excited beginnings. Resilience.
Fresh and glad welcome. Everything is possible.*

Mood: Inspiration
- Excite and inspire.
- Gather in, get-to-know.
- Tell a heroic story.
- Pump up expectations.

Mentoring Role
Keep watch on inspiration. What perks up the group and
each one in it? Discern the first sprouting of children's gifts.

Southeast

Activity: Energize Awareness

Natural Cycle: Morning/Seeding
*Movement, jump-starting rapid growth. Excited chatter.
Birds darting and begging.*

Mood: Motivation
- Orient and motivate.
- Energize, wake bodies and alert senses.
- Set the agreements, explain the plan.
- Take off running.

Mentoring Role
Keep an eye on making sure everyone is ready, harnessed,
and encouraged.

South

Activity: Foray

Natural Cycle: Noon/High Summer
Heat of the sun. Plants devour sunlight. Animals busy and curious. Hard work and surges of concentration. Teamwork and self-sufficiency.

Mood: Perspiration

- Focus and inquire.
- Go out on forays that take a lot of your program time.
- Play strategic long-lasting strategy games.
- Move through them like animals.
- Adventure and explore widely.
- Track, do research, collect and keep notes.
- Get down and dirty.

Mentoring Role
Challenge body, mind, and soul, fiercely and connivingly. Question and question again. Coach curiosity and endurance.

Take on the role of coach. Supervise them as if they were a work crew, teaching them skills they need, and nudging their endurance with praise and challenges. Mold them into focused teamwork.

Instill the Core Routines of questioning, tracking, field guides, and journaling. Whenever you can, be ever alert to training them as naturalists. Quiz them regularly! Do hard science.

Do some coaxing for the bewildered, and specialize for the intrepid.

Southwest

Activity: Wander

Natural Cycle: Afternoon Heat/Exhausted Summer
Hot, humid, out of breath in the heat of the day.

The work is done. Time for a nap. Relaxing, resting, taking care. Checking in, finishing up, internal growth.

Mood: Relaxation
- Relax and internalize.
- Take a break.
- Give individuals space and time.
- Let those who want to, play games.

Mentoring Role
When they grow weary, call for a break. Apply the 50-50 principle (see p. 18). A good time for adult leaders to talk about what they're seeing in the kids, and where they want to go from here.

West

Activity: Show & Tell

Natural Cycle: Sundown/Harvest
The sun lowers and sets, casting glorious light over the ripe fields and orchards. Animals finish their winter preparations. Bellies are fat. People come home to the fire, sharing news and processing their harvest.

Mood: Congregation
- Gather and share.
- Tell each other their Stories of the Day.
- Show off Finds and Map them.
- Debrief the human interactions of the outing. Enrich camaraderie, release tensions. Give thanks.
- Journal, sketch and glean field guides to elaborate glimpses.
- Enjoy Village Time. Linger longer with friends.

Mentoring Role
Walking along back with a grownup all to yourself is a treat for children. Engage with their stories while walking along with a kid or two. Set the seeds for reflection. Bring in some of your experience to point out heritage and heroics and their niche in it.

Be an Expert. Exclaim on the amazing science of the universe they met today. During "Village Time," look through microscopes or build a fire or carve or knit or snack together. Give them something to think about.

Discern and help everyone recognize their personal passions and styles, their natural born abilities. Led by your curiosity, guide them about their interests.

Northwest

Activity: Still, Quiet, Alone (Sit Spot)

Natural Cycle: Dusky Evening/Late Fall
Letting go, looking back, preparing for the future. Gathering in the final fruits and nuts and squashes. Halloween, darkness descends. Memories rise.

Mood: Reflection
- Release and reflect.
- Relive what connected you with nature today, the little deep gems.
- For short programs, this is the end. Send them off with blessings like dandelion puffs.
- For longer programs, this is a good time for going off Still, Quiet, and Alone to ponder, sketch and journal.
- If you have a Village, hangout making food, snooping the nature tables, practicing skills, devising camouflage, chatting.

Mentoring Role
See community dynamics as the story being told by the kids and their antics. Enjoy the plot, the setting, the characters, and sometimes tweak it to make it a better story.

North

Activity: Ceremony

Natural Cycle: Midnight/Winter
The still silence of a winter full moon. Roots and animals curled up asleep. Dormancy, distillation, clarity. Enduring dark and cold and curling up warm, sleeping, dreaming.

Mood: Integration

- Distill and integrate.
- Apply the lessons of the day.
- Turn short-term learning into long-term wisdom.
- Turn Core Routines into take-home habits.
- Honor turnings with rites of passage.

Mentoring Role
Mother Nature teaches in mysterious ways. Help Her along.

Enable Ceremony. The Elder in you, or an Elder from your village, may step in here.

Enable a sense of kinship with wild plants and animals. Invite respect, etiquette, awe, and reverence.

Northeast

Activity: Home Base (End & Beginning)

Natural Cycle: Pre-Dawn Transition/Thaw
End and beginning, death and rebirth, transition from one cycle to the next, a mysterious connection.

Mood: Regeneration
- End and beginning.
- Let go of the day, dream on it, and wake up with a new grip.
- Release, renew, restore. Let resilience sprout naturally.

Mentoring Role
Keep everyone in their senses and their gratitude. Create a safe, familiar, outdoor space, where you can hold an opening and closing circle, tell a starting story, and come together at the end for Show and Tell.

Encourage "ceremonial consciousness" in this space – keep it clean, dress it up, and encourage kids to use their best words, and listen with appreciation and respect to others.

Keep everyone in their senses and their gratitude.

SECTION 5
Raising the Natural IQ

Nature Connection is Education.

Information is pouring through the Amazonian bookshelves. And it shows that raising the Natural IQ is an urgently important form of education.

The Mind of the Mentor is spinning with theory.

- What am I really teaching?
- How can my teaching wake up awareness?
- How can I design my program?
- What is the course of activities for my people and place?
- Where in my schedule can I instill Core Routines?
- How can I justify my Invisible School as legitimate education?

This section has some abbreviated research about why this is learning, how it is science, and how you can implement it.

The last chapter, "Indicators of Connection," brings the book into a bundle with a proposal for standards for Nature Connection Education.

Chapter 16

The Outdoor Brain

The earth formed four and a half billion years ago. Elemental life began early, and for a long, long time it developed strategies for being alive in a chemical universe. Brains evolved at the center of mobile survival. Human brains came into being very recently, around 250,000 years ago.

We developed a very capable brain, the core of which navigated outdoors, because outdoors was what we did all day.

Human cognition evolved around this core brainpower to become a thriving species capable of affecting the fate of the Earth. The source of all information and memory and the engine coordinating our survival considerations was a robust brain.

Chronic indoor life has recently put some of our awareness, agility, critical thinking, and problem-solving skills to sleep. Nature Deficit Disorder is dumbing us down.

Let's wake up and hone that innate brainpower – its sensory awareness, its powerful memory, quick decision-making, strategic thinking, and its calculative and intuitive capacity.

Let's raise that Natural IQ so it can drive the context, the operating systems, of all higher level thinking. Let's bring fresh energy into our thinking process.

Here is some good information for how to do that.

Thanks to John Medina, author of *Brain Rules*, for inspiring this section.

Move Outdoors

Exercise the whole brain!

Problem solving while on the move – hunting and gathering, or fighting and fleeing among others in a continually changing environment – is what developed human thinking.

Our brain was born outdoors. The cerebral cortex of Homos Erectus and Sapiens developed while traveling on foot over challenging terrain for about 12 miles a day! They were moving, paying attention, and improvising.

Much of the brain's real estate is devoted to coordinating movement with the senses of sight, touch, hearing, taste, and smell. The tongue and thumb use a lot of brainpower.

Movement keeps the hungry neurons vital with oxygen flow, so they are toxin-free and actively growing.

Full range of motion develops eye-motor coordination, organ vitality, and skeletal agility.

Sensory awareness jumps to attention when moving outdoors, with all its feelers out, and the brain processes lots of information in a lively nexus.

Advice

Play games! Sneaking and stalking games, race and tag, explorations and adventures in all terrains and weathers. Keep them moving among challenges.

Excited Focus

Make learning emotional!

Intense learning happens when an adrenaline surge of interest meets directed focus.

When the new, the dangerous, the edible, and more, alert sudden strong attention, then neurons fire chemical messages across synaptic clefts creating a flurry of sequential processing.

- **First,** something captures emotional attention. Will it fight, flee, feed, or relate to me?
- **Second,** the brain retrieves what it already knows about it. Where have I seen this before?
- **Third,** it asks its higher reasoning powers if they need to pay attention.
- **If yes,** reasoning and hormones plunge in to pay sharp, close attention.

This focus is dense and alive with learning, even forging new neurons to grasp new information. It takes a picture that imprints permanently.

Advice

Hook brain interest with an emotional rush, then guide focused attention to elaborate the detail.

If a snake slithers by, follow it. If thunder roars, make shelter. If a bird calls an alarm, look alert.

To sustain that high-energy focus, shake up emotions again, and again. Every seven minutes! Because attention spans are very short and they need to be frequently recaptured.

- Look for opportunities to surprise an emotional rush.
- Change direction.
- Tell a strong story to rouse adventure.
- Ask intriguing questions.
- Put kids on the spot.
- Deprive and redirect attention.
- Be downright foolish to capture interest.

Good Stress

Stress, in moderation, is good.

Stress enhances learning. Stress and pleasure are both manifest by an aroused physiological condition which motivates lifted spirits. What's the difference between good stress and bad stress?

If the stress is a challenge and you can act on the hormone rush – exercise the heightened blood pressure, quick reflex muscle, and sharp focused attention – it greatly enhances learning and problem solving, and it's thrilling and memorable.

If, however, the stress is so overwhelming that you shut down in fear, aversion, or powerlessness, then it's bad stress, and best avoided.

Advice

Play games. Race and compete. Tag and escape. Scout and ambush. Pretend to be lost. Build shelters and pretend to be safe!

Bring attention to "hazards" as good stressors. Use both real risks and perceived risks deliberately.

> "Is that poisonous?"
>
> "It's rattlesnake season."
>
> "Maybe a bear is watching us!"

Begin a foray with a challenge that gives it meaning and purpose. An important errand, a hunt, a much-prepared-for expedition.

Monitor stressors wisely.

Get to know your students' comfort zones, as individuals and as a group. Choose to push their edges but not freeze them down or freak them out. Be prepared to put some time and attention into individuals at the fringes.

Wandering is Learning

Make time to wander.

Wandering means all the things we do during time-out, breaks in the action, stopping for a rest together, puttering around, outbursts of free play, sitting on a log watching, going to check something out – these are exactly how we learn.

Yes, we need unstructured time.

Wandering is the most active learning of all. The relaxed, unfocused brain follows its own drummer as its background processing reviews, considers, remembers, and invites new ways of seeing things.

Learning absorbs and digests before it settles down into long term memory. Breaks after long periods of focus allow for reflection, review, integration of ideas and feelings that have just happened.

Advice

Take a Break. Wander Off. Do it. Allow it. Schedule time for it.

This is so hard for teachers. If you are a principal, give your teachers a workshop on how to take a break and then provide resources that enable them to! Advocate for it, because it's good education.

Repeat to Remember

Repeat to remember and remember to repeat.

Remember
There are many kinds of short and long-term memory – conscious and unconscious, images and words, dreamy gists and their spreadsheet details.

When we experience anything,

- First we "get the gist."
- Which includes an emotional tone.
- Through repetition, detail falls in.
- A network of related impressions builds up.
- The "gist" becomes "elaborate."
- And memory imprints.

Repeat
Remember and forget, remember and forget. To anchor a solid memory, it needs to pass through short-term memory about five to seven different times, in five to seven different contexts.

- Have a striking learning experience.
- Think about it later, recall its fine points.
- Write it down. Tell it to somebody.
- Remember it when it comes up in a different context.
- Dredge it up from memory when you need it to solve a different issue.

NOW it's embedded in long term memory.

Advice

Encourage storytelling, journaling, and sketching, to wrap experience into words, to pinpoint insights, and to impress images and patterns.

Chapter 17

Sensory Wiring

We are wired for keen sensory awareness.
Hunting and gathering, on two legs with tools and in communities, developed a strategic brain, one that combined acute sensory awareness with critical thinking. Adapting to changes boosted the stakes and we became curious talking animal scientists.

The brain starts all its thinking with the senses.
Five (and many more) senses are primed to ripen with use. There are whole lobes to process vision, interpret touch, translate sound waves, coordinate movement, and absorb tastes and smells.

All our senses are a kind of radar.
They pick up vibrational signals about what's around and ahead. Activating this radar stretches our senses, reaches our roots, and reveals wondrous discoveries.

Advice

Just pay attention to awareness on your outings with kids.

- **Stop, look, and listen** at every opportunity.
- **Teach them HOW** to use their senses and hold them accountable for practicing.
- **Have spot quizzes** and contests to see who noticed what.
- **Pull apart specimens** and eye them with a looking glass.
- **Study Amazing Animal Senses** and peruse field guides that show the anatomy of nostrils and eye sockets and muscles.
- **Imagine how** insects and fish and birds perceive and navigate their worlds. Imitate them.

The Five Senses

We learned as toddlers, then again as high school biology students, how our senses work. Here's a quick reminder course in how the brain manages its senses *(with special thanks to Diane Ackerman, author of A Natural History of the Senses).*

The EYE: See wide, see focused

With eyes astride our noses, humans can see half a sphere, near and far, with predator vision. It's by far our dominant sense, 70% of our sensing is visual and much entwined with movement.

Our lens keeps moving things in focus. Our muscular iris is a light meter. On our eyeball wall, rods see black and white widely, and cones detect color and detail in tight focus.

Vision is by far humans' best sense. Visual analysis in the brain takes many steps.

- **The retina assembles photons** into little movie-like streams of information.
- **The visual cortex processes** these streams, some areas registering motion, others registering color, etc.
- **Finally, we combine** that information back together, and we see what we see.
- **Visual processing** is greatly intertwined with motor processing. We see on the move, ever re-focusing.

The EAR: Hear roundly

The ear is a delicate contraption with receivers, decoders, and transmitters. What it hears are vibrations – sound waves in varying amplitudes and frequencies. Hearing translates sound from all directions and makes meaning out of it.

It's hard to locate the origin of sound. Cup your hands behind your ears to make Deer Ears and scan to triangulate where sound is coming from.

The NOSE: Smell warmly

Nostrils are tropical olfactory channels full of waving hairs of cilia grabbing actual molecules of smell that pass through.

Smell is older than words and goes straight to the heart of the brain. There are very few straight-up words for smell or its related sense, taste, because they are so primordial.

The TONGUE: Taste sharply

The tongue tastes sweet at the tip, sour on the sides, salty around the front, and bitter at the back. Bitter warns of poison.

The SKIN: Touch softly

Skin is like a grass field of nerves for pressure, heat, and vibration. Cheeks, lips, soft skin and fingertips feel the most. Skin feels electric current, tastes chemical traces, absorbs pressure, and relaxes into warmth.

There are two ways to feel with the skin

- **One is to stand there** and feel the air, humidity, breeze, weight of clothing, sun on cheek, spots of body heat, temperature of feet on ground – the feelings that enfold your whole body in space. "I feel hot. I feel rain coming..."
- **The other is to use** hands and fingertips to examine the texture, weight, glossiness, heat, wetness, size – of what you see... "The leaf feels sticky. I feel a tick under my dog's fur."

Sensory Wiring

Imprinting Images

Sensory information pours in from everywhere and meets in the brain where it assembles into an imprinted image – not words but pictures – of sights, smells, sounds, tastes, and feels.

Face-to-face, eye-to-eye, fingers-to-dirt encounters produce the best images. We learn and remember and communicate most wholly through direct experience.

Patterns of shape and light, and video images of movement and sound, build up into an organic vocabulary of "search images," – what field biologists use to spot things in the wild.

Attended to, this pattern recognition can lead to seeing principles, hypothesis-testing, and the laws of higher physics.

Here's how these images imprint into memory

- **When an image has been glimpsed,** it leaves a bright, scattered glow in the brain.
- **When it is seen again and again,** the picture gets colorful and nuanced, includes movement and texture.
- **When it is sought for,** recorded, drawn, and examined, it becomes a sophisticated piece of nature vocabulary.

Telling Stories

When they are wrapped in stories, images root into long term memory. Put the crystal snapshots of the senses into words, into stories, little narrative memories, replete with time and place and people, that record key identifying features, cues of body language, twinges of emotion.

Telling these stories, out loud, to a community who listens, is the best of all ways to imprint the images.

Hearing yourself say what you say in public ceremony is amazing! Saying what you say, fully present to the memory in body, mind, and soul, makes a great story.

Telling a story as performance entails acting out body movements and voices, which embeds the memories even deeper.

Imitating

Practice animal movements. There is no better way to get under the skin of a thing than by copying its movements! Do imitation warm-ups and play games of Race and Tag or Hide and Sneak to get kids' whole bodies and senses into it.

Make animal sounds. Use crow calls and wolf howls to call and gather, imitate varied bird calls, bark, grunt, and snort!

Practice animal perceptions with games like Scent Trails. Listen with Deer Ears for bird alarms, go out for blindfold experiences that challenge finding the trail with your feet, and night walks that put all sense perceptions on alert, just like nocturnal animals.

These full body imitation activities speed all our sensory imaginations through roller coaster learning curves.

52 Senses

When you get the gist, or have an inkling, a medley of senses is probably involved. Intuition seems to be a function of many-faceted attention.

The Sixth Sense may be any combination of the obvious five, and many more, plus a little magic. Think about our potential for awareness!

Thanks to Michael J. Cohen, in *Reconnecting with Nature,* for his elaboration of 52 senses. Here are a few of them.

> » Sense of appetite and hunger.
> » Sense of temperature and temperature change.
> » Sense of season, including the ability to insulate, hibernate and winter sleep.
> » Humidity sense, to find water or evade a flood.
> » Sense of vibration, resonance, sonar frequencies.
> » Sense of one's own visibility and camouflaging.
> » Sense of proximity.
> » Sense of fear.
> » Sense of play.
> » Sense of excessive stress.
> » Sense of emotional place, of community belonging.
> » Psychic capacity, foreknowledge, intuition, instinct.
> » Spiritual sense, conscience, capacity for sublime love, sense of sorrow, and sacrifice.

**Stimulating more of the senses together
at once develops intuition.**

Chapter 18
Nature Literacy

Coyote excites, Mentor guides, but Nature Teaches.

With enhanced natural intelligence, students learn to read the Book of Nature.

The Book of Nature has no beginning and it has no end. "It's an untidy evolution of leapfrogging, photosynthesizing, fighting, fleeing, and reproducing life!" says the writer David Rains Wallace. It tells a long story that is ever changing and has interesting morals!

The bits and pieces add up to a core of knowledge and an appreciation of the interdependent ecology of all things, including our human selves.

Reading the Book of Nature entails learning nature's language, digesting a vocabulary, gaining fluency in search images, listening for context, and following etiquette. Once they learn to read, kids begin to decipher for themselves nature's storylines.

Advice

Focus on the topic of the present experience, whatever is in your face. Get to know one place well, one species, one ecological concept. Question, investigate, and experiment with it.

Teach fundamentals of how nature works so kids can hang their findings on a storyline. How the sun works. How water flows. How rocks got there. How life cycles. How diversity interacts.

Converse in appropriately scientific language. Let young children invent names and urge older students to learn Latin classifications. Log findings and do experiments following protocols.

Finish up with reports. Literate people not only read and talk, but they also research and experiment and write conclusions, stories, and proposals about their findings.

Science

The sciences run all the way through the Book of Nature: Geology, Physics, Chemistry, Biology, Thermodynamics, Meteorology, Hydrology, Dendrology, Botany, Zoology, etc.

And if your children's reading involves farming, hunting, fishing, geo-caching, photographing, trail-building, restoring, cultivating, or survival, then the engineering, social, and political sciences kick in too.

For the teachers among us, science is likely to be an important goal of your outings. There is nothing better than a serious science project to justify outings and engage kids' sustained focus.

With younger kids or casual outings, just get them started with scientific awareness and a habit of hypothesizing and testing.

With older children in ongoing programs, use field guides, science texts, GPS devices, and all the digital capabilities at your command to investigate, calculate, and map.

Chapters of the Book of Nature

Any outing is enhanced by a topic of study, an integrating theme. To impose a little order on all this diversity, it helps to organize programs and assess learning following some natural groupings as an object of study.

Here are the Chapters of the Book of Nature from *Coyote's Guide to Connecting with Nature*. The big book expands on these with species lists and learning goals and resources.

The sequence follows the flow of the seasons from young beginnings to sophisticated ends. These are the Natural Science categories that you can take on one at a time, or a little bit of all at the same time!

Chapters of the Book of Nature

East *(Sunrise/Spring)*: **Hazards:** A Call to be Alert and to Use Common Sense. Plant, animal, water, and weather Hazards.

Southeast *(Morning/Seeding)*: **Motivating Species:** Things to Catch, Eat, Climb, and Tend. Fish, frogs, snakes, bugs, berries, fruits, rocks, trees, gardens. Vital interactions.

South *(Noon/High Summer)*: **Mammals:** And Other Hard to See, Yet Totally Track-able Critters. Track and sign of animals and others. Investigate clues, monitor changes, keep track.

Southwest *(Afternoon/Summer)*: **Plants:** Nature's Grocery Store and Medicine Cabinet. Edible, medicinal, and craftable plants. Wandering and browsing along the trail. Making cordage and salves. Tasting the wild.

West *(Sundown/Harvest)*: **Ecological Indicators:** How it All Works Together. Landmark features, historical markers, topography, waterways, larders and lacks.

Northwest *(Evening/Late Fall)*: **Reverence Species:** Relics of the Ancestors. Rocks, trees, springs that have been operating there a long, long time. Indigenous history.

North *(Midnight/Winter)*: **Trees:** Tools of Human Survival. Canopy for wildlife. Timber for shelter. Wood for fire and tools. Tall-standing survivors of many seasons. Survival through dark and cold winter.

Northeast *(Dawn/Thaw)*: **Birds:** Messengers of the Wilderness. Voices of baseline and alarm in vocalization and action. Flight patterns and bird calls. Uplifting spirits.

Chapter 19
Indicators of Nature Connection

Imagine your kids, raised outdoors by you this way:
They shine, there is a brightness in them, a sparkle in the eye, a jump in the joint, along with an easy way of being kind, a capacity for quiet attention.

Let's grow children like that.

Connecting, intimately, with wild nature is the educational goal of all this foolishness and wisdom, this awareness, these routines, these games.

How do you measure the outcomes? What have they learned? How do they show it? Let us choose outcomes perhaps different from the norm, ones that matter to us.

Here are the Indicators of Connection: Eight Standards to aim for. You can teach to these, be aware of obstacles in their way, and be the Mentor who guides children through their learning curves.

- ✓ Common Sense
- ✓ Aliveness & Agility
- ✓ Inquisitive Focus
- ✓ Caring & Tending
- ✓ Service to Community
- ✓ Awe & Reverence
- ✓ Self-Sufficiency
- ✓ Quiet Mind

Common Sense

Direction: East *(Sunrise/Spring)*

Standard:

* **Learns** from experience, nature smarts
* **Sensible** choice-making
* **Cautious** but not fearful
* **Practices** good hygiene - reduce, reuse, recycle
* **Respectful.** Listens before knocking
* **Comfortable** outdoors

Obstacles:

» **Obliviousness** to surroundings and impacts
» **Carries** cultural fears
» **Lack** of experience with boundaries
» **Fear** of new things

Advice:

* **Correct** "old wives' tales," Nature's mostly safe
* **Introduce** the hazards of the hood
* **Teach** them basic how-to guides
* **Coax** them through the edges of fears

Aliveness & Agility

Direction: Southeast *(Morning/Seeding)*

Standard:

   * **Truly alive**, sparkle in the eye
   * **Physically** quick and agile
   * **Glint** of mischief, flash of daring
   * **Whole** hearted

Obstacles:

   » **Lack** of physical strength
   » **Fear** of doing what you're not supposed to do
   » **Lack** of confidence, sadness, loneliness

Advice:

   • **Dare** to be the go-between who explains to parents why they are muddy
   • **Wink** at glimmerings of fear and excitement and give them the go-ahead
   • **Subtly allow** weaker kids a startup advantage, others will understand

Inquisitive Focus

Direction: South *(Noon/High Summer)*

Standard:

* * **Bright** curiosity, inquisitive focus
* * **Wholly** absorbed, intense
* * **Nature**-smart-scientific
* * **Exploring**, questioning, persevering

Obstacles:

* » **Concrete** mind, may be good at who, what, where, when, but not ready for why and how?
* » **Impatient**, frustrated, wanting answers
* » **Bored**, "wish-I-were-home with my games"
* » **Gives up** easily
* » **Overwhelming** know-it-all

Advice:

* • **Ask** level one questions, what they already know. Figure out their starting points
* • **Time** the giving of clues or answers to meet the edges of their active curiosity
* • **Sidle** up to individuals to coax their searches
* • **Get** the know-it-alls to fall in the swamp and quiet down because they're wet and muddy and miserable!

Caring & Tending

Direction: Southwest *(Afternoon/Summer)*

Standard:

* * **Tenderness**, caring and tending
* * **Empathy**, protection, encouragement
* * **Grounded**, centered, emotionally comfortable
* * **Stand up** for common decency
* * **Tend** faithfully

Obstacles:

* » **Gear-adrift.** Careless with equipment, water, possessions, lunch
* » **Doesn't know** when to stop and exhausts self
* » **Thoughtless** of others

Advice:

* • **Invite** self-awareness
* • **Steer** kids to include each other
* • **Teach** and role model basic self-care
* • **Assign** care-taking roles for the good of all
* • **Challenge** self-sufficiency

Service to Community

Direction: West *(Sundown/Harvest)*

Standard:

* **Appreciative**, generous, connected and contributing
* **Comfortable** with own gifts to the group
* **Other**-centered
* **Enjoys** connection with the human community

Obstacles:

» **Doesn't know** what to offer
» **Introverted** and uncomfortable with groups
» **Over** bright with ego! Domineering
» **Self-centered**

Advice:

* **Set up** regular tasks to train service skills
* **Call out** individuals for tasks they're well fitted to
* **Come together** with thanks for those who helped

Awe & Reverence

Direction: Northwest *(Evening/Late Fall)*

Standard:

* * **Open** to being stunned, speechless, awestruck
* * **Respectful** of wild things
* * **Wonder** in presence of something bigger than self
* * **Aware** of connection with the wild world
* * **Sense** of humility, sacred responsibility

Obstacles:

* » **Noisy** mind, can't quiet down
* » **Embarrassed** by tenderness
* » **Limited** by cultural stereotypes

Advice:

* • **Encourage** the capacity for wonder with silence at the spur of magic moments
* • **Tell** impromptu stories about the deep history of the universe
* • **Develop** a reverence for lineage and their niche in it

Self-Sufficiency

Direction: North *(Midnight/Winter)*

Standard:

* * **Meets** challenges with clarity, calm
* * **Flexible** wisdom and true personal power
* * **Adapts** to the flow of life
* * **Ingenuity**, creativity, leadership
* * **Hope**, resilience

Obstacles:

* » **Fear** and falling apart in hard times. Emotional panic
* » **Lack** of confidence/skill to deal
* » **Real** pain, weakness, incapacity, confusion
* » **Follower**-mind. Care for me, tell me what to do

Advice:

* • **Attend** to safety first
* • **Be there** to pick up the pieces, but let them fall apart
* • **Pair up** kids whose combined skills can cope
* • **In low-risk** situations, put followers in the lead

Quiet Mind

Direction: Northeast *(Dawn/Thaw)*

Standard:

* **Unobtrusive** receptivity, intentional invisibility
* **Belonging**, at home in nature, quiet kinship
* **Finding** fit, knowing home
* **Empathy**, imagination
* **Humble**, well-rounded, patient

Obstacles:

» **Fear** of wildlife, fear of wilderness
» **Family** mind, not ready to embrace larger tribes
» **Easily disturbed**, over stimulated, can't get quiet

Advice:

* **Encourage** them to greet new things with curiosity and trust, not judgment
* **Provide** authoritative ceremony to quiet them down.
* **As they** become able, employ Sit Spot often
* **Help** them be insightfully, even reverently, thankful

SECTION 6
Coyote's Ripples

Start your own Coyote Mentoring program.

Create good trouble. Splash up some ripples.

Turn the tide!

Chapter 20
Our Story

Ellen and Lexie wrote this book because they recognize the powerful value of the Coyote Mentoring approach and want to promote and advance it. Their vision is that every child everywhere gets access to the experience of deep kinship with wild nature. With this pocket guide, they throw a pebble in the pond, hoping it will fan out in ripples of ever-widening Coyote programs.

They are both teachers, Ellen taught private high school and college English with an adventurous edge; Lexie got a Masters in education, taught secondary science, then homeschooled two girls all the way up.

Ellen Haas loved Coyote Mentoring the moment she met it. She and Jon Young and Evan McGown, conspired for many years to get the Art of Mentoring practice into print by writing *Coyote's Guide to Connecting with Nature.*

Lexie Bakewell is a long time curious naturalist. She thrives on poking around outdoors; then combing through field guides to know more about who she met on her wanders. Her background in field biology and Science Education make everything interesting.

Mackenzie, Lexie's daughter, is an artist and author who was raised in nature. As the publisher of *Coyote's Pocket Guide*, she put into practice the Coyote Mentoring techniques to coax and focus the two to keep writing until the book was complete.

Chapter 21
Glossary

Book of Nature

A vocabulary of search images and knowledge that enables one to understand what is happening in the natural world. It is the story of who, what, where, when, why and how, that makes up our encounters in the natural world.

Core Routines of Nature Connection

Fundamental practices to enhance nature connection that are introduced, then repeated every day in every way, until they make up the core of your curriculum. These are practices that can be incorporated in every aspect of life – for the rest of your students' lives.

Coyote Mentoring

An outdoor teaching strategy developed and tested for many years by Jon Young, Wilderness Awareness School, and worldwide Eight Shields organizations. Passed on orally through Art of Mentoring workshops, the strategy was written into the big book, *Coyote's Guide to Connecting with Nature*, in 2008, and now this little book makes it pocket sized.

Invisible School

The subtle and invisible schooling that occurs when Coyote spices things up and Mentor guides from behind. The kids don't know they are "learning," but in fact, they are accumulating through stories and dirt time, an enormous familiarity with their environment.

Natural Cycle

The framework for designing a lesson plan, or a longer curriculum, based on the natural energetic flow we all know from experience – as each day cycles from sunrise to high noon to sunset to sleepy night, or as each year cycles from spring to summer to fall into winter. It makes common sense to guide student outings along the same natural flow.

Natural Intelligence

Humans have inherited from their forebears the extraordinary potential to perceive subtle details, to notice colors, smells, tastes, patterns, changes, sounds, designs, movement. When our innate senses are honed and developed they are called our Natural Intelligence.

Nature Connection Education

Connecting with Nature is educational. Simply by playing in the midst of diverse and dynamic processes of nature, children develop knowledge, skills, abilities, and most importantly, a felt sense of kinship with the natural world

Nature Literacy

Learning to read the Book of Nature, which enables one to observe and interpret what is happening in the interdependent web of life.

Turning the Tide

What Nature Connection Education can achieve if we stir up bold ripples and engage more and more children. We can turn the tide on Nature Deficit Disorder and change the direction of environmental degradation, not because we have to, but because we love to.

We hope this book inspires you to start your own Coyote program. It can be anything from taking your own children outdoors, to gathering your friends for a forest walk, to leading nature games in your classroom, to sustaining a year-long program with neighborhood kids, homeschoolers, scout groups, afterschool care, or anything else.

A Coyote program is a way to adapt your schedule to the natural cycle, to use the teachings of Coyote in your everyday life. Make it your own, call it a book club, a nature group, a classroom activity, a team bonding outing, whatever fits your site and situation.

As the Coyote Mentor and leader of your Coyote program, you are both the wily trickster and the wise mentor. Enjoy the experience and spark curiosity and connection to nature in your wake.

" By tending the wild
we are tamed to be wild. "

ZieBee Media
PORTLAND, OREGON, USA

Made in the USA
Coppell, TX
08 March 2024

29908467R10079